What's Wrong With This Picture?

Yosemite National Park

Fictitious, erroneous, silly, dangerous and strange pictures of and about Yosemite National Park

by Scott N. Tipton

Copyright © 2012 Scott N. Tipton

All rights reserved.

ISBN-10: 0615536867   ISBN-13: 978-0615536866

Library of Congress Control Number: 2012934721

Dedication

This book is dedicated to my loving wife, Barbara, for putting up with my many faults, among them expending a fortune on Yosemite related collectables and ephemera and my spending hours at a time on the computer writing this book.

(Oh yeah, she came up with the idea for the title.)

CONTENTS

	Introduction	v
	Acknowledgments	vii
Part 1	Bears, Deer, Elk, Bison & Mountain Lions	1
Part 2	Glacier Point – Getting There and Showing Off	88
Part 3	Misplaced and Misidentified Features	150
Part 4	Improvements by Destruction and Distraction	200
Part 5	The Odd, Strange and Silly	228
	Afterthoughts	261

Introduction

This book is the result of my love for Yosemite National Park. I have an absolute passion for the place. Ever since my first visit in about 1959, Yosemite has always been one of my most favorite places on earth.

My family would visit the park every few years and we would always camp. Going to Yosemite was a true adventure for me – sleeping in a tent, hiking the trails, going fishing, cooking outdoors, the nightly Ranger programs at the campgrounds or Camp Curry, the campfires at night and, of course, the Fire Fall. And I especially loved the waterfalls. They fascinated me.

My last visit to Yosemite as a young person was probably in 1969 at the age of fifteen. Some things had changed in those ten short years, or at least it seemed that way. It was really crowded! I don't know if it actually had grown more crowded or I was just more aware of it. But it was still an adventure and I enjoyed almost every minute of every visit.

It would be twenty more years before I would come to Yosemite again. It was in the spring of 1989 with my wife Barbara. We were married in 1987 and this was our belated honeymoon. We camped out, did the usual tourist activities and had an absolutely great time. Being there also really invigorated me. I was a different person than I was at home in San Diego. I just couldn't sit still. I wanted to go everywhere and see everything.

This is also where the roots of this book got its start. I bought my first "Yosemite" book – *JOHN MUIR – THE EIGHT WILDERNESS-DISCOVERY BOOKS*. It included *My First Summer in the Sierra*, *The Mountains of California*, *Our National Parks* and *The Yosemite*. It was fascinating reading and I learned a lot from John Muir's writings.

Barbara and I would visit again the following spring, again camping out. On this trip I would buy two more books – *ADVENTURES OF A MOUNTAIN MAN – The Narrative of Zenas Leonard* and *WESTERING MAN – The Life of Joseph Walker* by Bil Gilbert. Both of these books contained accounts of the first known "Americans" to have crossed the Sierra Nevada Mountains in the Yosemite vicinity. I was now hooked not just on Yosemite but on its history as well.

We have visited Yosemite almost every year since then. And my collection of books about Yosemite grew. I acquired books by Lafayette Houghton Bunnell, J. Smeaton Chase, Galen Clark, Francis P. Farquhar, Ansel F. Hall, Richard J. Hartesveldt, Alfred Runte, Carl Parcher Russell, and, of course, Shirley Sargent and Hank Johnston, just to name a few.

My collecting soon branched out to other things. And, thanks to eBay®, it became an obsession. I was buying (and still am) anything and everything related to Yosemite's history – old postcards, stereoviews, maps, travel booklets and brochures, advertisements, *Yosemite Nature Notes* and more books.

As I collected, I started to notice in some of the books there were pictures of things that were odd or different or incorrect. The same thing was true with the postcards, stereoviews and other ephemera. I found these pictures very amusing and soon I was looking for and buying these types of things specifically. I soon realized I had accumulated quite a large collection of the odd, incorrect, silly and incredibly dangerous pictures all pertaining to Yosemite.

I felt that this collection would make quite an interesting study. And thus, we have this book. I hope you find this collection of pictures as amusing, interesting and educational as I have.

ACKNOWLEDGMENTS

I would like to thank the following individuals for their help and cooperation in the writing and compiling of this book:

William "Bill" Bruce; Tom Bopp, musician and Yosemite historian; Dr. Paul P. Clark, *Adams Art* - researcher-collector-writer on Ansel Adams & Yo Semite; Linda Eade, Librarian, Yosemite Research Library; Eldon Grupp and Susan Cramer, collectors and archivers of everything related to Yosemite; Ed Herny, President of the San Francisco Bay Area Post Card Club; Hank Johnston, Yosemite historian and author; Ted Orland, photographer, educator and author; Tom Philips, Board Member of the Mariposa Museum and History Center.

And very special thanks to my friend Barbara Lawrence and my wife Barbara for proof-reading the manuscript and their helpful editing suggestions.

PART 1

BEARS, DEER, ELK, BISON & MOUNTAIN LIONS

AN IMPORTANT CAUTIONARY NOTE:

IN THE FOLLOWING SECTION OF THIS BOOK ARE NUMEROUS PICTURES OF PEOPLE FEEDING BEARS AND DEER. SUCH DEPICTIONS DO NOT IN ANY WAY CONDONE THE FEEDING OF WILDLIFE.

THE RULES AND REGULATIONS OF YOSEMITE NATIONAL PARK REQUIRE THAT VISITORS RESPECT ANIMALS AT A DISTANCE. IT IS ILLEGAL TO FEED OR APPROACH THEM. KEEP YOUR DISTANCE FROM ANIMALS, EVEN IF THEY APPRAOCH YOU. FAILURE TO OBEY REGULATIONS MAY RESULT IN A FINE OF UP TO $5,000.

Postcards from author's collection.

Here are two postcards both published circa 1950. The publisher(s) is unknown; however the pictures are almost definitely taken by the same person.

Either the photographer stumbled upon a one in a million photo opportunity or things were rigged in the composition of the pictures.

This bear cub didn't just happen to be sunning himself on a tree stump when the photographer appeared on the scene. A closer examination of the postcards shows that this poor animal wasn't at the right place at the right time by pure happenstance.

A close-up detail of the photos shows how the scenes on the postcards were possible.

If you notice in the detail on the right, you can see what appears to be a rope or chain leading from the bear cub and running down and wrapping around the tree stump, tethering the poor guy in place.

In the detail on the left, it isn't as clear that something is tethering the cub to the stump, but there definitely is what appears to be a collar around the bear's neck.

Many used other means to obtain pictures of animals, either appearing to be candid and natural scenes, or posed for that special souvenir snapshot. The most popular, of course, was to tempt the creature with food.

Mistreating a wild animal or even tempting one with food, just for the sake of a photograph or artwork, is terribly exploitive. Doing it for the sake of making money is just plain wrong and a crime against nature.

How would you like it if someone were to tie you to a tree, a rock or some other immovable object just to get that "perfect picture"?

Photo from author's collection.

Postcards from author's collection.

Having already identified how this bear cub was positioned against its natural tendencies to pose for the perfect photograph, we have another example of the same postcard.

The postcard on the right is how the scenery should appear (except for the bear cub). The postcard on the left is the picture you get when the publisher is unfamiliar with Yosemite Falls and its environs (or dyslectic) and makes prints with the negative placed backwards in the print and development equipment.

But I've seen several of these backward postcards for auction on online. So, either no one ever noticed or really cared.

Postcard - **"Chief Ranger Townsley, With His Pet Bear Cub"**
Western Publishing & Novelty Co., Los Angeles, Calif.
From author's collection.

Pictured here is Forest S. Townsley and he was one of the nine "First Rangers" of Yosemite. He came to Yosemite as a ranger in 1913 and was made the national park's Chief Ranger in 1916 after the establishment of the National Park Service. He served in that position until his death in 1943. He is buried in the Yosemite Valley Pioneer Cemetery.

While having his picture taken with his "pet" bear cub and then making it into a postcard may have been cute, it certainly gave the wrong message. No, it is not O.K. to keep bears as pets or feed them publicly for fun, even if you are the Chief Ranger. People and bears should not interact in close proximity, especially when food is included in the equation. (By the way, the bear cub's name was "Prunes".)

In 1933, when this particular postcard was mailed, visitors to Yosemite had a totally different experience with the woodland creatures than what is allowable today. Even though signs were posted saying not to feed the bears and other wildlife, literature stated should not do so *by hand*. Park employees and visitors saw very little wrong in feeding wild animals as long as one was careful.

The impact of people's attitudes, including park officials, towards wild animals can be seen when reading the message written on the back of this postcard by the young girl that mailed it –

> Dear Junior, I saw two little baby bears in Yosemite with their mother when I came up last month with some friends. This time we saw only big ones. *I had my picture taken with one standing on his hind legs.*
> From, Cousin Rachel
>   (*Italics mine*)

That's O.K. honey. Go stand next to the nice big bear so daddy can take your picture. Smile pretty!

Photographs from author's collection.

Didn't they have laws against child endangerment back in the 1930s?

People wanted to get as close as possible to the wild animals in the National Parks, including the bears. If that meant tempting them with a piece of food to draw them closer, then that's what they were going to do. And the enticement to do so was even greater if it meant getting your picture taken with the beast.

Now if you were to see people like rangers, naturalists and Park Superintendents feeding bears, deer and other wild creatures; or pictures of them doing it, aren't you going to assume it's O.K. for you to do so as well? Not so long ago, in Yosemite as in many National Parks, this was what almost everyone did.

In this picture, left to right (standing), Arthur C. Pillsbury, resident Yosemite photographer and owner of the Studio of the Three Arrows/Pillsbury Pictures; Harry Cassie Best, resident Yosemite photographer & owner of Best's Studio (and Ansel Adams' father-in-law); Virginia Best Adams (Mrs. Ansel Adams); Mrs. Dolbow; (kneeling) Bertha Dolbow.
From YOSEMITE: Saga of a Century, 1864 – 1964
© 1964, The Sierra Star Press, Oakhurst, California

This photograph appeared in the official visitor's guide "YOSEMITE NATIONAL PARK - CALIFORNIA" (United States Department of the Interior, National Park Service. United States Printing Office, Washington [D.C.], 1934). The caption reads: *"Children find many new friends in the park."*

This same booklet, in the section RULES AND REGULATIONS, had the following information: "**Warning About Bears.** – Do not feed the bears from the hand; they are wild animals and may bite, strike, or scratch you. They will not harm you if not fed at close range."

So, apparently you *COULD* feed them as long as you weren't too close to them??

Here are some more pictures of park officials doing what was acceptable before the full impact on the animals, ecology and people visiting our National Parks was understood.

Superintendent Horace Albright sitting at a table with black bears.
Photographer unknown; No date.
National Park Service Historic Photograph Collection

This man sitting at the table with three young black bears is Horace M. Albright. He was Superintendent of Yellowstone National park from 1919 until 1929. He was not only superintendent during this time period, but he was also Assistant Director, Field, of the National Park Service and in charge of all national parks west of the Mississippi River. In 1929 he was appointed Director of the Park Service and served in that position until 1933. This made him Chief Ranger Forest Townsley's bosses' boss. (Read it again, it makes sense.) If this man thought it was alright to feed and play with the bears, it certainly must have been something anyone else could do if they wanted.

Enid Michael, NPS ranger naturalist offering a bear a beverage.
National Park Service Historic Photograph Collection.
Catalog Number: HPC-000207

Enid Michael was a NPS ranger-naturalist at Yosemite from 1921-1942. While she was primarily interested in botany, she was also very interested in birds. During her twenty years as a "temporary" ranger she collected plant specimens, created the wildflower garden behind the Yosemite Museum, took visitors on nature walks, gave lectures at museums and wrote a total of 537 articles about Yosemite; more than anybody else.

With all of that practical knowledge about nature, she apparently did not think that large bears were too dangerous to share a beverage with. (It looks like a beer.) This bear obviously had had too much close exposure to humans.

Since this was the normal activity with bears by public figures in the Parks, visitors would follow suit given the opportunity.

"The bear cubs are the clowns of the forest."

Photo by A. C. Pillsbury*

I don't know for sure who this gentleman is, but it appears to be Chief Ranger Townsley again. It is an extremely cute picture, like the postcard of Ranger Townsley and the bear cub on his shoulder. But feeding wild animals such as this created more problems than it solved and set the wrong example.

Most of the problem was people's lack of understanding of the balance between man, animals and the rest of nature. Unbalancing one part of the way nature was meant to function unbalanced the rest of the natural environment.

***Lights and Shadows of Yosemite** Being a Collection of Favorite Yosemite Views, Together With a Brief Account of Its History and Legends, For Those Who Want to Know and Enjoy Yosemite More by Katherine Ames Taylor.
Published by H. S. Crocker Company, Inc., San Francisco. Copyright, 1926, by Katherine Ames Taylor

Prior to the time period when feeding and other interaction with wild animals within the National Parks had reached this point, the bears, deer and most other wild creatures had been over-hunted. The California state mammal, the grizzly bear, had eventually been hunted to extinction. Since people who visited the National Parks, like Yosemite, expected to see wild animals, things had to change. The laws that protected animals from over-hunting were finally better enforced and new laws were passed. Feeding the animals was just a way to help visitors have a better National Park experience by being able to see them up close, even if it was detrimental to them.

The clowns of the forests are the bears. In Yosemite the bears have amused visitors with their antics for many summers. Since dogs, cats, and firearms have been prohibited in the Park, the bears have become extremely friendly with humans. They have learned to beg for candy and to knock on the doors of cabins for handouts. The visitor with patience and some molasses chews can almost always prevail upon a bear to pose for a snapshot. The Yosemite bears emerge from hibernation early in the spring with large appetites but with an instinct which tells them to abstain from food offered by humans until they have rooted around for herbs and roots that they require. Later they are in the market for sweets. Visitors are advised not to feed bears from their hands.

Excerpt from *The Yosemite Trip Book*
Copyright 1926 by F. J. Taylor, Published by H. S. Crocker Company, Inc., San Francisco

What's Wrong With This Picture? - Yosemite National Park

Feeding bear cubs in Yosemite.
Photos courtesy Tom Philips, Board Member of the Mariposa Museum and History Center

All photos from author's collection.

The Union Pacific Railroad launched a campaign in the 1920's to advertise its trains to West Yellowstone, Montana. They decided to produce a series of posters featuring caricaturized bears to entice vacationers to travel by train to visit Yellowstone National Park. The railroad hired "bear artist" Walter Oehrle (or variously Oeable or Oerhle and pronounced EARLY), a Chicago artist/cartoonist, to do the artwork for the posters.

Walter apparently preferred to do preliminary sketches using live subjects rather than photographs.

Here is Walter in Yellowstone employing one of his solutions to the problem of getting a model to pose -

Bear artist with bear. (Artist is Walter Oeable, of Omaha, NE), Yellowstone National Park, ca. 1933.
Photographer: George A. Grant.
National Park Service Historic Photograph Collection. Catalog Number: HPC-000603; Other NPS Image Numbers: Wa. 1070a

Union Pacific Railroad Travel Promotion Poster for Yellowstone National Park.
By Walter Oehrle.

As illustrated in the poster above, those cute, playful bear cubs are "all lined up" as if expecting you to show up and have fun with them. The poster may have been a promotion for Yellowstone, but the expectations were the same in most of the National Parks where there were bears, deer and other large, "friendly" animals to be easily observed.

This postcard was made for the Yellowstone market as well, but it reinforces what was being marketed to the public at the time.

Postcard - © by Asahel Curtis for Northern Pacific Ry. Co.
C. T. American Art Colored, Chicago / Quality Line, Bloom Bros. Co., Minneapolis, #Y. P. 34 / 91070
From author's collection.

The caption on the back of this card reads:

SETTING THE TABLE FOR BEARS AT LAKE CAMP, YELLOWSTONE PARK.
The bears are very amusing, interesting, and companionable, many of them, also voracious eaters. Quite mannerly at table - sometimes. Always ready to eat.

Wild bears are "companionable"? As in congenial? I don't think so.

Of course, people weren't just feeding the bears. Visitor information published by the National Park Service, park concessionaires and park naturalists routinely listed the best areas to see and feed the deer, squirrels, chipmunks, etc. The Glacier Point Hotel was once one of the favorite places to have "tame" mule deer eat out of your hand. It created great photo opportunities.

Judge Walter Fry Feeding Deer in Giant Forest – Sequoia National park
Photograph by Lindley Eddy
THE NATIONAL PARKS PORTFOLIO, Sixth Edition
By Robert Sterling Yard; Revised by Isabelle F. Story, Editor, National Park Service
UNITED STATES GOVERNMENT PRINTING OFFICE, WASHINGTON: 1931

The gentleman in this photograph, Walter Fry, became a park ranger in Sequoia and General Grant National Parks in 1905, when the U.S. military had jurisdiction over the parks. By 1910 he was Chief Ranger and when the Army gave up supervision of the National Parks in California, he became Sequoia/General Grant National Parks' first civilian Superintendent. He became "Judge" Fry when he was appointed U.S. Commissioner, or Federal Judge in those parks. He helped start the first Nature Guide Service in the National Parks.

But, here again is a high ranking park official, though doing what he thought was a perfectly kind act, actually setting an improper example.

Park Naturalist Bert Harwell offers a tidbit to a friend, April 5, 1930.
Courtesy of the Yosemite National Park Research Library
National Park Service Historic Photograph Collection

Both the previous photograph as well as the next one are also found in the book *YOSEMITE: The Embattled Wilderness* by Alfred Runte (©1990, University of Nebraska Press.)

The very sad irony of feeding wild animals is that they are perfectly capable of fending for themselves and always have survived without man interfering unnecessarily. Offering food to the animals to get closer to them, or feeding them thinking that they need food from humans for survival can create drastic consequences.

Ranger Bill Reyman with a herd of Yosemite Deer, ca. 1930.
Courtesy of the Yosemite National Park Research Library.

In the case of the feeding of deer alone, while it was not frowned upon and almost everyone did it, the outcome was often a very sad one. In *YOSEMITE: The Embattled Wilderness* the caption for the photograph of "Ranger Bill Reyman with a herd of Yosemite Deer" is extremely upsetting:

> In Park Service reports, deer grown tame from being fed by tourists were often called "beggar" or "pauper" deer. Most such animals, like "garbage" bears, were quietly captured and killed. Quite obviously, the Park Service itself was also to blame for feeding and spoiling wild animals.

These deer had become dependent on receiving handouts from park employees and the thousands of visitors. They were conditioned to not fend for themselves .

Sadly, while not as widespread a problem now as it was a few decades ago, it is still an issue. Park visitors are becoming more and more "Bear Aware" so incidents with bears and other animals have grown fewer each year; however people do still feed the cute little forest creatures.

Feeding deer is not as large a problem as it used to be, but some folks continue to do it for that photo opportunity or just to get close to them. Progress is evident by the fact that most deer in Yosemite will avoid contact with humans. Still some are not above walking up to you looking for that handout. That means that they have been habitually fed by hand.

I had a personal incident a few years ago in Yosemite Village in front of the village store while waiting for a shuttle bus. A young buck walked up to me expecting some sort of treat. As I just stood there not responding, he lowered his head and impolitely nudged me in the ribs with his antlers. If I had been a forty pound little child instead of a 210 pound adult, the outcome could have been very bad.

Let's not let scenes like this become the norm in our National Parks again.

Don't feed the animals! Keep wild animals wild!

Photo from author's collection

Photo from *The Yosemite Trip Book*
Copyright 1926 by F. J. Taylor
Published by H. S. Crocker Company, Inc., San Francisco

Photos from author's collection.

What's Wrong With This Picture? - Yosemite National Park

Photos from author's collection.

Photos from author's collection.

What's Wrong With This Picture? - Yosemite National Park

Photos from author's collection.

Do not feed the squirrels, chipmunks or birds either!

Postcard - Pillsbury Picture Co., 174 Geary St. San Francisco.
From author's collection.

Postcard - Camp Curry Studio, In the Yosemite National Park.
From author's collection.

Postcard - **"Yosemite Bear"**
From author's collection.

Postcard - **"Native Sons, Yosemite National Park, California."**
Pacific Novelty Co., San Francisco & Los Angeles
From author's collection.

All four of the postcards on the preceding pages have something in common. The common factor is a lot more obvious in the second, third and fourth cards. All of them show these lovable black bears rooting through piles of trash and garbage.

Why would anybody want a picture keepsake or postcard to mail to friends and family of bears digging around in the garbage? Because, for a very long time, the best places to see bears were where the garbage was dumped. And since very little garbage was hauled out of the park to landfills and garbage dumps as we know them today, there were garbage dumps in several places in Yosemite itself, and they attracted a lot of bears.

The first postcard shown is by the Pillsbury Picture Co. and was published circa 1910 to 1915. This information was written on the back of the card by the original owner:

> "These bears come out of the mountains and down near the camp to feed. People sit around the place for hours waiting for them to come."

The National Park Service website for Yosemite under the link for "Nature & History" and under the heading "Nature - Black Bears" has this information:

> Perhaps no more than five bears co-existed within the granite walls of Yosemite Valley prior to the settlement of non-native people. But after more settlers and visitors began to live in and visit Yosemite, it was common to see as many as 60 bears at a time rummaging through garbage at a popular spot called [the Bear Pits]. Back then, Yosemite bears were fed by rangers. The visitors who photographed them saw the bears as being synonymous with the park, and the bears themselves were quick to learn that human contact meant food.

Another source* explains that this situation soon grew into a large problem:

> The increased visitation to Yosemite caused a variety of natural-resource related problems, not all of which concerned fire protection, meadow degradation, or river control. Attracted by campers' foodstuffs and the ever-expanding park garbage pits, bears began to make nightly camp raids. A barrage of visitor complaints prompted the National Park Service to begin a bear scrap feeding program in an effort to lure them away from visitor use areas. This basically comprised government institutionalization of a practice already followed by some of the early hotel owners as a popular form of visitor entertainment.

The Yosemite National Park Service website, again under the link for "Nature & History" under "Wildlife - Bears" gives us this information:

> The history of interactions between humans and black bears in Yosemite is a long one, marked by some periods that we now look upon as shameful. Early in the park's history, little was done to keep bears from becoming conditioned to human food. Garbage was readily available in developed areas, and little was done to discourage visitors from feeding bears. Indeed, the National Park Service maintained several "bear pits" in the park where bears were fed garbage in an attempt to keep them out of park campgrounds and lodging areas, and to provide visitor entertainment.

*Historic Resource Study - YOSEMITE: THE PARK AND ITS RESOURCES - A History of the Discovery, Management, and Physical Development of Yosemite National Park, California by Linda Wedel Greene, September 1987, Yosemite National Park / California

A garbage pile somewhere in Yosemite Valley in the 1920s.
Photo from author's collection.

Notice how obese this bear has become from eating the leftover scraps of human food.

Not a pretty picture.

Bears rooting through a garbage pile somewhere in Yosemite Valley in the 1920s.
Photo from author's collection.

Can you believe that this was a normal sight in Yosemite Valley before the 1950's?

As early as 1917, the official Department of the Interior booklet "*Rules and Regulations - Yosemite National Park*" had the following map of Yosemite Valley showing where the "official" Bear Pits were located. (There were others near campgrounds and lodgings not on the map, such as near Camp Curry and the Glacier Point Hotel.)

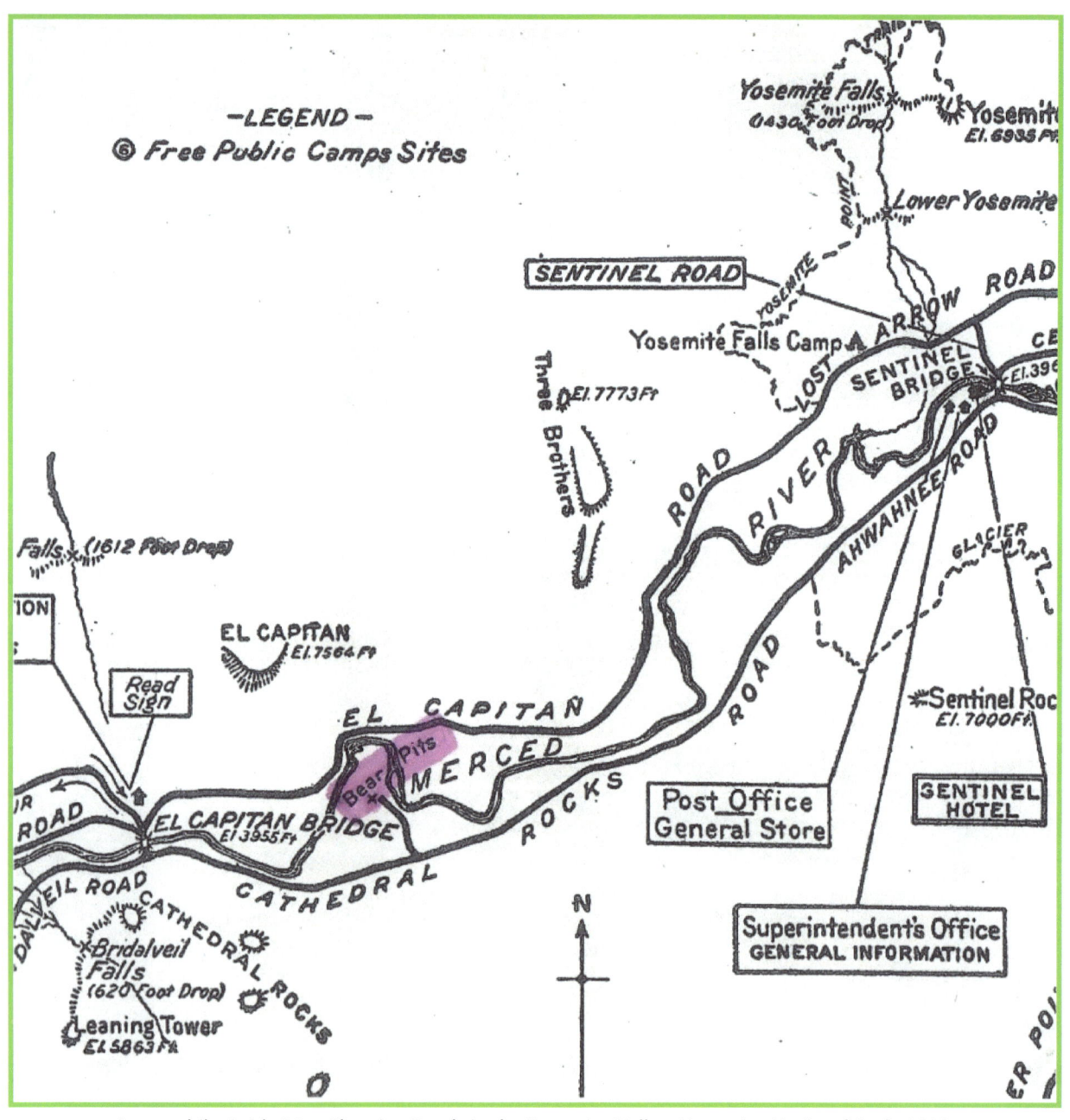

Automobile Guide Map Showing Roads in the Yosemite Valley, Yosemite National Park, 1919.
From author's collection.

Yosemite Valley's bear feeding pit – July, 1932.

Photos from author's collection.

The plan to put garbage and trash in specified areas as "pits" or "platforms" did not work out as intended though. In fact it backfired as this feeding program made the bears more reliant on human food and they became bolder in their begging for it.

Postcard - **"ANY SUGAR TO-DAY?" AT BEAR PITS, YOSEMITE, CALIF.**
Photo by D. J. Foley.
From author's collection.

The source cited previously (page 33) continues:

Knowing that they would be fed later in the day, bears began hanging around near the garbage pits during the day, begging from cars along the main park highways to fill the time between feedings. In 1923 the Yosemite National Park Company built a special feeding place for bears near the Merced River bank a mile below Old Yosemite Village. Hundreds of visitors collected there every night to watch the bears eat and play on an electrically-lighted platform. Park Service rangers even began putting on interpretive programs there in the evenings before the bears ate. By the early 1930s, bear feeding had become one of the summer's prime attractions.

Photo from author's collection.

Photo from author's collection.

Again, the National Park Service website for Yosemite under the link for "Nature & History" under the heading "Nature - Black Bears" has this additional information:

> In the 1920s and 1930s, human-conditioned bears were beginning to wreak havoc, injuring tourists and raiding restaurants nightly. In 1925 [or 1923], the National Park Service began luring bears away from restaurants and campsites with a trail of food scraps leading to open pit garbage dumps. This bear feeding program also attracted tourists who wanted to view bears close up. Responding to visitor demand, the National Park Service then designated a parking area and constructed bleacher seating at the dump in Yosemite Valley.

Even the Chief Naturalist of the National Park Service, Ansel F. Hall, made this sanctioned feeding of the bears in a designated area sound like a good idea since the National Park provided protection from hunters and the bears "learned that they can live here without being afraid . . ."

In his book *YOSEMITE VALLEY an Intimate Guide*[*] he wrote:

> The BEAR PITS . . . are not far from the main road and may be reached by an inconspicuous motor way which branches to the left from the highway. Yosemite is one of the very few places in California where the American Black Bear, one of the most interesting and valuable citizens of the forest community, is afforded protection from the so called "sport" which some men seem to find in killing him with a high powered rifle. Park bears have learned that they can live here without being afraid - indeed, with advantage to themselves, as is attested by the occasional pilfering of sweets from a car or camp or by frequent visits to the "Bear Pits" where choice bits of garbage lend a variety to a menu unknown to their fugitive and less civilized brothers. During the summer two or three bears will usually be found here during the day; generally, however, sleeping in the lower branches of the trees round about. From dusk until midnight one can be almost certain of seeing half a dozen or more.

Today, going to Yosemite, or any other National Park, and expecting to be entertained by sitting on bleachers at night in a well lit arena listening to a park naturalist explain the natural history and habits of the bears while feeding them is entirely out of place. But back in the 1920's and 30's this was part of the National Park experience and how you got a good close look at the animals.

*YOSEMITE VALLEY An Intimate Guide by Ansel F. Hall, Chief Naturalist, National Park Service Illustrated by Leo Zellensky. Copyright June 1929 by the National Park Publishing House, Berkeley, California

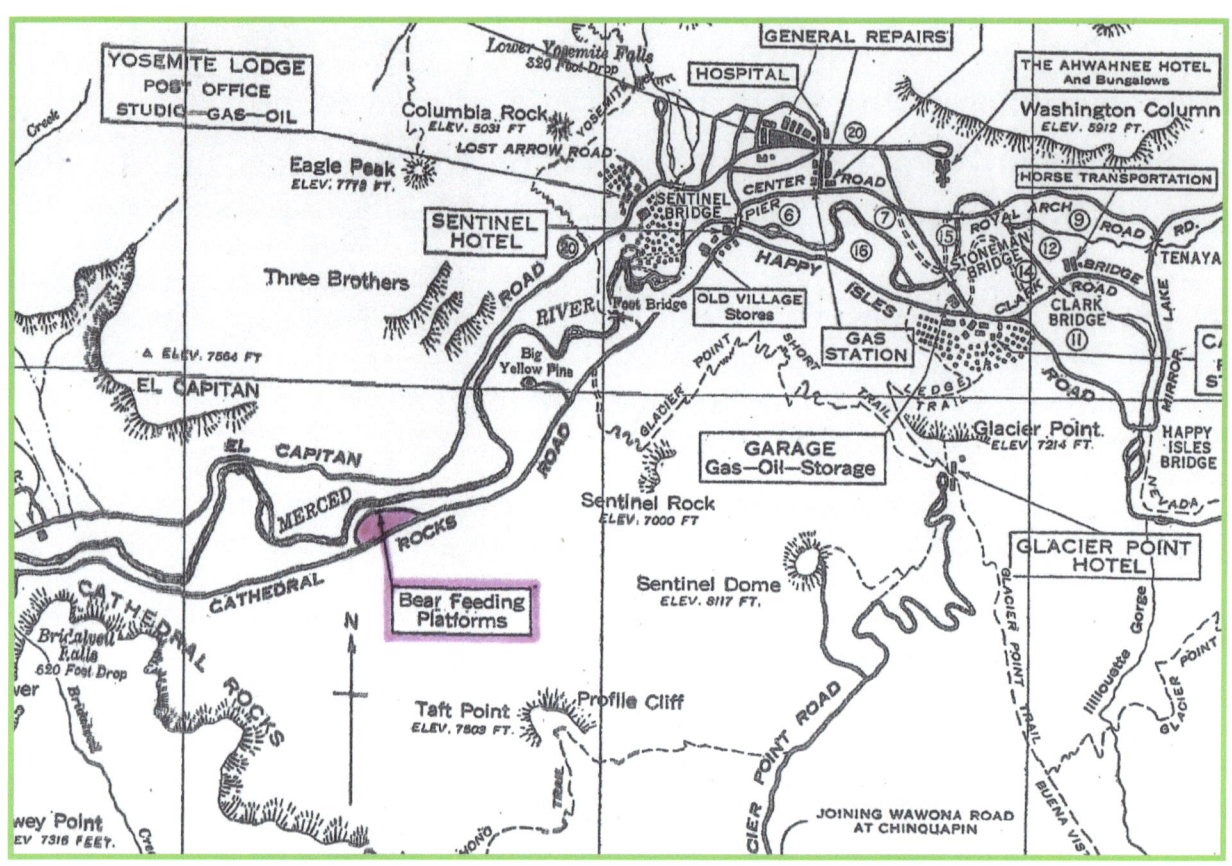

Automobile Guide Map Showing Roads in Yosemite Valley
Circular of General Information Regarding Yosemite National Park -1931
Notice how by 1931, the "Bear Pits" of 1919 had become the "Bear Feeding Platforms"
From author's collection.

But, this was no real solution. The cited National Park website continues with just one result of the bears being fed at the platforms – "Bear related injuries increased as people made attempts to get too close."

Watching the bears being fed was one of the summer's biggest attractions, like the Firefall. It was even announced in the daily activities programs.

```
                        Yosemite National Park
                        Office of the Superintendent
         GOVERNMENT NATURALIST PROGRAM FOR WEEK BEGINNING SEPTEMBER 8, 1930


   AUTO CARAVAN- Floor of Valley  3 p.m. daily except Sunday

        Park at Museum any day at 3 p.m.  A Naturalist will lead the group,
        stopping to explain points of especial interest.
        Monday- Wednesday- Friday- Western end of Valley
        Tuesday- Thursday- Saturday- Eastern end of Valley

   LECTURES

        BEAR PIT each evening at 9:30-- Park Naturalist
             Two miles down south side river beyond Old Village

        THE AHWAHNEE  Tuesday 8:30--8:55 p.m.
             "Animals of Yosemite"  C. C. Presnall, Asst. Park-Naturalist

        YOSEMITE LODGE  Wednesday 8:15-- 8:45 p.m.
             "Birds of Yosemite"  C. A. Harwell, Park-Naturalist
                    Friday  8:15--8:45 p.m.
             "Indian Foods and their Preparation" Geo. Crowe, Asst. Park-Naturalist

   MUSEUM

        Open daily 8 a.m.--to 5 p.m.
        Geology Lectures -  10:30   11:30 a.m.
                             2:30    3:30 p.m.
        Indian Demonstration back of Museum.


                                              C. A. Harwell
                                              Park-Naturalist
```

This is a copy of a mimeographed schedule for the "GOVERNMENT NATURALIST PROGRAM FOR THE WEEK BEGINNING SEPTEMBER 8, 1930".
The first lecture listed is *"BEAR PIT each evening at 9:30 - - Park Naturalist."*
From author's collection.

In the official visitor's guide "YOSEMITE NATIONAL PARK - CALIFORNIA" (1934) under the heading FREE EDUCATIONAL SERVICE it states: "The bears are fed every evening at 9:30 o'clock at the bear pits, and a short talk is given on animal life of the Yosemite."

The government sanctioned feedings only made things worse for both the bears and the humans. Bears were getting too greedy and demanding, and people were getting injured. During one year alone, the hospital in Yosemite Valley treated sixty injuries to tourists due to bear related incidents.

Postcard - **"'I Like Sugar, Too.' At Bear Pits, Yosemite, Calif."**
From author's collection.

Just an example of how accustomed to being in close proximity to people and how brash the bears had become is the notation written on the back of this postcard by the original owner –

This is a picture of one of our playmates – no fooling either – they come right in your tent after sundown looking for food!

Yosemite Valley black bears eating garbage, November 1942.
Photo Courtesy of the Yosemite Research Library.

Glacier Point garbage dump.
Photo Courtesy of the Yosemite Research Library.

It was soon realized by some scientists and naturalists that feeding the animals in specific designated spots, on the one hand to lure them away from certain crowded areas, but on the other hand to get closer and better "interact" with them, was not working out. It just created another bad set of circumstances. The caption on the next photograph taken from a 1932 study of human and animal relationships was this:

"When unarmed people invite intimacy with a large powerful animal, such as the black bear, injuries are sure to result."

Photograph taken November 3, 1929, in Yosemite Valley. Wild Life Survey No. 22
Photo by Joseph S. Dixon. Taken from *Fauna of the National Parks of the United States – A Preliminary Survey of Faunal Relations in National Parks*, by George M. Wright, Joseph S. Dixon and Ben H. Thompson.
Contribution of Wild Life Survey, Fauna Series No. 1 – May, 1932. United States Printing Office, Washington [D.C.], 1933.

Trying to feed wild animals, even with the best of intentions, does not always work out well.

The large number of bears and the large numbers of people were bound to start getting on each other's nerves. Careless visitors began to resent being scratched or clawed as they tried to feed the furry beggars and the valley hospital staff kept busy each season binding the wounds resulting from this interplay. Bears became less a "cute" attraction and more of a pest to the visiting public. In an attempt to reduce the accident rate and reintroduce the bears to wild food gathering, the Park Service prohibited feeding, teasing, or molesting the animals. The valley, however, simply did not contain enough natural resources to feed the number of bears living there. Also, as long as the pits and camp foodstuffs were available, the bears had no intention of moving on, and visitor-bear contact continued to pose problems.

Eventually the Park Service perceived the bears, which had lost their fear of man, as a significant threat to visitor safety. Coupled with an increased awareness of Park Service responsibilities for the preservation of wildlife in its natural state, this resulted in a phasing out of the scheduled, interpreted feeding of bears in the fall of 1940. At that time rangers also began trapping bears and moving them out of the valley.

The Park Service's practice of dumping garbage in open pits and the later inadequate solid waste collection program resulted in an increase in black bear population numbers, wider distribution, and in continuing alterations of their natural wild habits. Even after bear feeding stopped, camp foodstuffs continued to attract bears, leading to property damage and personal injuries, resulting in turn in destruction of some bears and constant relocation of others. Efforts to prevent man-bear conflicts have consisted of public education, removal of artificial food sources, enforcement of bear feeding regulations and proper food storage; control of problem bears, and continuing research on black bear population dynamics and their interrelationship with humans.*

*Historic Resource Study - YOSEMITE: THE PARK AND ITS RESOURCES - A History of the Discovery, Management, and Physical Development of Yosemite National Park, California by Linda Wedel Greene, September 1987, Yosemite National Park / California

Yosemite bear feeding area, location unknown.
(Bottom - Close-up detail with warning signs.)
Courtesy of the Yosemite Research Library.

Warning sign circa 1943.
Photo from author's collection.

These days in Yosemite an aggressive program warning visitors not to feed the bears and to keep food entirely unavailable to wild animals is gradually reducing negative interactions. The numbers show that damage caused by bears seeking human food is way down from just a few years ago.

The best policy now is to keep wild bears wild. And not just the bears. Everyone should work hard to keep all wildlife wild.

A postcard mailed in 1956.
Notice that the warning implies that you could feed the bears as long as you were not too close to them.
From author's collection.

By the 1950s, the National Park Service had finally become very serious about not allowing the feeding of wildlife.
This is the type of flyer you would receive upon entering a National Park when I was a youngster.
U.S. Government Printing Office: June 1957 – Form 10-108 / O-428004
From author's collection.

Postcard - Western Publishing & Novelty Co., Los Angeles, Calif., 338 / 3A-H154
From author's collection.

After the summer of 1940 the bear feeding "show" was stopped because of the multiple problems it created for both the bears and the park visitors.

But of course postcards of bears were popular and sold well. So what did the publisher of this postcard do when the park policy about feeding wild animals changed? They simply changed the caption from *"'ANY SUGAR TODAY?' AT THE BEAR PITS"* (see page 38) to *"HOWDY FOLKS"*.

It's not really that clever, but *"I CANT **BEAR** TO LEAVE YOSEMITE"* and *"**BEARLY** able to write"* were already taken.

Postcard - **Big Bear, Yosemite National Park, California.**
Scenic View Card Co., San Francisco, Cal.
From author's collection.

Somehow on this postcard by another publisher the same bear is there and the trash was kept in the picture. In fact the trash really stands out. But the big tree that was on the other very similar postcards (pages 38 and 52) just disappeared.

What in the world happened to that big tree?

The "zoo" in Yosemite Valley, 1922.
Photograph by Rev. LaRue C. Watson.
Courtesy Yosemite Research Library

For many visitors to Yosemite the wildlife was nothing more than a source of amusement and they expected to see wild animals, one way or another. Beginning in 1918, in an effort to please and appease these visitors, the National Park Service allowed the setting up of a "zoo" or "menagerie" in Yosemite Valley.

As can be seen in the photograph of the "zoo", it was nothing more than a collection of metal wire cages.

The "zoo" began with the display of three orphaned mountain lion cubs whose mother had been killed by the State Lion Hunter in the Wawona area. Soon a bear cub was added and then another. By 1920 the "zoo" was a featured item in guide books and maps.

In the book *GUIDE TO YOSEMITE - a Handbook of the Trails and Roads of Yosemite Valley and the Adjacent Region*, by Ansel F. Hall, U.S. National Park Service, In charge of Information, Yosemite National Park (Copyright 1920 by Ansel F. Hall) is found this information:

> North of the Merced and about a third of a mile from the center of the village is the schoolhouse and a group of other government buildings. One of these is the menagerie and contains several wild animals captured in the region. The chief exhibits are a pair of California mountain lions, and a number of bear.

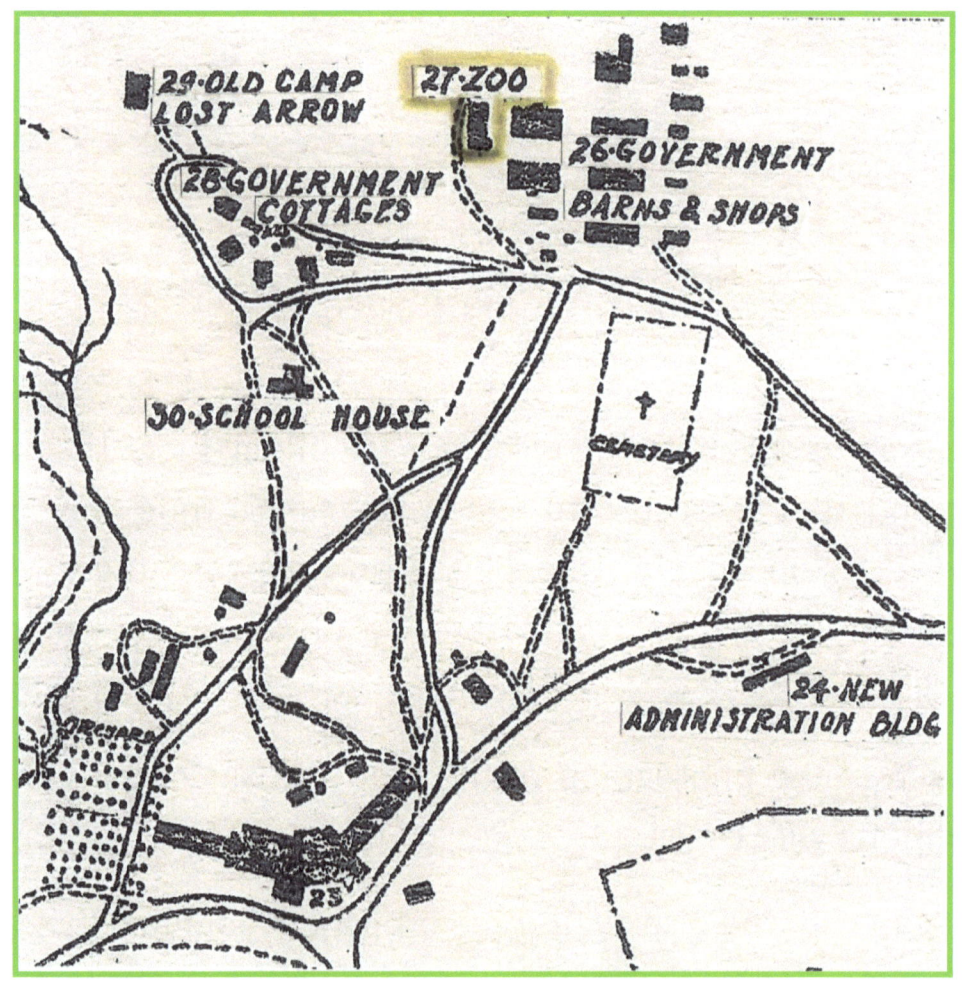

Section of "Map of Yosemite Village" from
GUIDE TO YOSEMITE - A Handbook of the Trails and Roads of Yosemite Valley and the Adjacent Region
Zoo shown at top center.
Map labeling altered by author for easier identification.

Apparently by 1922, something had happened to two of the three original mountain lion cubs and there was another one on display in the cages:

MOUNTAIN LIONS MAY HE SEEN IN ZOO

Too [sic] splendid examples of the Mountain Lion, the largest member of the cat family found in California may be seen at the Zoo near the government barns. The darker colored one is a female that was reared from a kitten captured near Wawona. The lighter colored one, a male, was secured from Yellowstone National Park. The Mountain Lion is an enemy of the deer and the state offers a substantial bounty for scalps and hires a mountain lion hunter who rids game refuges of this animal.
  Yosemite Nature Notes, Volume I, Number 5, August 7, 1922

While the *Guide to Yosemite* stated that the "menagerie" contained "a number of bear" there were apparently only two bears permanently caged and on display. By the end of 1923 it was decided that they should be set free. The Park Service had built the bear feeding platforms, so bears were very easy to see there every night.

Plus the caged bears had grown extremely large - "these two bears weighing about 800 pounds each were costing the government too much for food, and that a cut in the budget of several hundred dollars a year could be effected just by turning Billy and Brownie out to forage for themselves."

The *Yosemite Nature Notes*, Volume II, Number 16, December 31, 1923 gives this insight:

Zoo Bear Prefers Captivity

Early this month the order was given that "Brownie" and "Billie," the two caged Yosemite bears, be given their liberty. For five years this pair has assured all visitors a sight of a Sierra bear. Now, with bears at every hand, it seemed best that the zoo give up "Brownie" and "Billie."

When the impounding bars were removed, "Brownie," the little female, lost no time in leaving her prison. She made great leaps for the forested talus nearby and for the first time in five years she stretched her limbs in a good high tree climb. "Brownie," by the way, was captured in a tree on that same talus slope.

But "Billie" was of quite a different opinion as to where the winter should be spent. In the cage is a den dug deep into the rocks, and there he has spent most of his hours of late. Each day a good friend brings gunny sacks full of choice kitchen leavings from which he may take his pick. For three days and nights after his untamed mate had deserted him, "Billie" stuck to his cage. And all this time the steel door stood wide open.

Billie was finally coaxed out of his cage with food –

> A pull on the rope slammed the steel door at his rear, and the bear found himself locked out of his home. He sniffed about the bars, ambled over to the side nearest his beloved hole, determined the impossibility of entering, and finally walked away dejected. That evening he returned and whined like a dog, clawing at the bars. A resident near the zoo declares that "Billie" returns each night and feeds from a garbage can that stands very close to the old bear den.

The two bears were so accustomed to receiving food from their keeper instead of scrounging for it themselves that a year later it was reported that:

> Robert Selby, who for several years cared for "Brownie" and "Billie," two Yosemite zoo bears that were liberated last spring, found that the animals came from their rock den for food every day of the year.
> *Yosemite Nature Notes*, Volume IV, Number 1, January, 1925

With the two bears gone, the two mountain lions were still on permanent display, and they still brought great interest by visitors:

EXPLANATORY LABEL PLACED WITH CAGED LIONS

The great interest of visitors in the mountain lions of the Yosemite "zoo" has led park service officials to post the following explanation on the lion cage:

CALIFORNIA MOUNTAIN LION
Felis oregonensis californica

ROCKY MOUNTAIN LION
Felis oregonensis hippolestes

The smaller lion in this cage is a female California mountain lion from the Yosemite Region. She is one of three that were captured as kittens by Jay C. Bruce, near Wawona in April, 1918.

The larger animal is a male Rocky Mountain lion, captured in Yellowstone National park about 1918.

No other American mammal has so wide a range. It is found from Canada to Patagonia, from the Atlantic to the Pacific.

Mountain lions are known as cougars, panthers and pumas. They do not attack human beings but are destructive to deer. Each adult lion may be expected to kill one deer each week. Fortunately they are not numerous; probably less than 20 lions range within Yosemite National park. It is evident that lions and other predators have not levied upon the Yosemite deer population in excess of their recuperative powers.

Lions are so wary that they are seldom seen except when trailed and treed by dogs. Many persons have lived in the mountains for years without seeing one. Human beings are in no danger of attack from mountain lions.
   Yosemite Nature Notes, Volume VI, Number 6, June, 1927

THE ZOO

It is the policy of the National Park Service not to keep animals in captivity except when they can seldom or never be seen wild. Bear and deer may be seen by almost anyone, but there is one extremely interesting large mammal which is so rare as to be unknown except by hearsay even to most old mountaineers. This is the California Mountain Lion, Cougar, or Panther which timidly shuns civilization and travels almost entirely by night. A pair of these handsome animals is kept at the Yosemite Zoo—about five minutes walk to the northwest from the Museum.

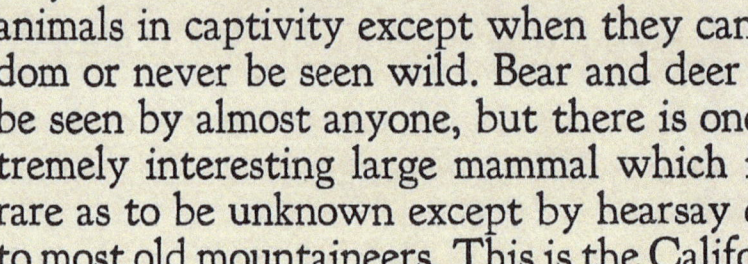

From *YOSEMITE VALLEY - An Intimate Guide*
By Ansel F. Hall, Chief Naturalist, National Park Service
Illustrated by Leo Zellensky
Copyright June 1929 by the National Park Publishing House Berkeley, California

Also, almost six years later Billie the bear was still showing that he had been permanently habituated to dependence on humans for food. In 1929 it was reported that on one July evening when the black bear "came for his regular evening cleanup of the garbage pail", he was in for a special treat:

> Billy was greeted cordially by the men who planned to give him a treat that he would never forget and, at the same time, test the eating capacity of a big hungry bear. The volunteer cooks soon had hot cakes covered with syrup coming in a steady stream from the kitchen stove to the back door where Billy was waiting. After exhausting the supplies, the cooks, and even the bear, a final check showed that Billy had consumed seventy-two flapjacks. At the finish he was seated on the ground, groaning and fairly gasping for breath, probably indicating a feeling of both pleasure and pain.
>
> This interesting eating exhibition shows the remarkable ability of the black bear to adapt himself to the presence of man.

Showing that he remembers the kind treatment and the delicious food he had received while in captivity, Billy still comes down every evening promptly at 6 o'clock to the cookhouse to get the choice leftovers, otherwise known as the "swell swill of the valley."

Yosemite Nature Notes, Volume VIII, Number 10, October, 1929

The "zoo" was finally abolished in November 1931 but when that happened, it had a very sad, ironic ending. It was feared that the two mountain lions still kept caged there would not be able to readapt to living in the wild after being hand fed for almost fourteen years. They were killed and the State Lion Hunter turned their pelts in to collect the bounty it was felt he missed out on when he captured the original three cubs.

In 1933, the buildings and cages that had become to be known as the "zoo" in Yosemite Valley were demolished.

Photograph courtesy William "Bill" Bruce and Tom Phillips

Once, either beginning in the late 1880's but at least by 1890, one of the attractions at the Wawona Hotel was a caged "Alaskan Bear", a large sub-species of brown bears.

Why the bear was put there, how it got there and how long it was on display are all mysteries. I suppose, if you want to give the visitors to your hotel a novel item to look at, it might as well be a big brown bear.

I could find only one reference to the bear in any old literature, a travelogue/guide book. Even this author seemed a bit perplexed:

> Supper is served at the Wawona Hotel, where we spend the night. This place has its own attractions in the shape of a fine water-fall, a lake, a trout-stream, Hill's picture gallery, and an Alaskan bear in a cage near the river.

It may seem strange that a bear should be imported from Alaska to the Sierra, which has plenty of its own. But they are less easily caught here, and avoid the haunts of men. We saw none on the way, nor any other animals except squirrels and a few birds, among which the pretty but unmusical bluejays predominated.*

The picture below shows the bear cage from a little later prospective. It's just to the left of the general store.

Photograph provided by Tom Bopp.
The Bancroft Library. University of California, Berkeley.

It's just another piece of strange, unexplainable history that happened in and around Yosemite. I'm sure that it seemed like a good idea at the time.

*THE PACIFIC COAST SCENIC TOUR - *FROM SOUTHERN CALIFORNIA TO ALASKA, THE CANADIAN PACIFIC RAILWAY, YELLOWSTONE PARK AND THE GRAND CANON* by Henry T. Finck. COPYRIGHT, 1890, BY CHARLES SCRIBNER'S SONS.

Postcard from author's collection.

I don't know why, but this postcard just really amuses me. It looks like this bear is really reading those trail signs. I mean, just look at the guy! Something is going on in that brain of his.

I always imagine he's thinking things along these lines:

"Where was there more food last time? Tenaya Lake or Glen Aulin?"

"Dang it! I'm on the wrong trail again."

"Hey! I don't remember this thing being here yesterday."

"Hold it a minute! I think I've been walking in circles."

"I thought it was closer than that! That's just too darn far. I'll go there tomorrow."

"Eeny, Meeny, Miney, Mo . . ."

"Idiot humans!"

"Waterwheel Falls? Sounds like fun."

"You know, it's always farther than the sign says it is."

"Fred said he was going to leave me a note saying where he was going. Now what?"

And another thing – If bears **can** read, how come they can't figure out how to break into the vending machines in the park? I know they know there's tons of food in those things.

What's the deal with that?

Postcard - *"The Ahwahnee – Yosemite Nat'l Park"*
Photo circa 1927 to 1933. Postcard available for sale as late as 1942.
From author's collection.

Isn't this a nice pastoral scene on this postcard - a photo of two deer lying in front of the beautiful Ahwahnee Hotel? The problem is this is not a scene anyone would have seen when visiting the newly built hotel under normal circumstances. These are not the mule deer usually seen in Yosemite. These are elk.

Not that you could not have seen elk in Yosemite Valley, for there was a brief few years when you could have. But the Yosemite area was not their natural habitat.

In 1921, the National Park Service accepted a small herd of twelve of the nearly extinct Tule elk (*Cervus canadensis nannodes* or *Cervus elaphus nannodes*, also commonly known as dwarf elk or California valley elk). The elk were placed in a fenced paddock of twenty-eight acres of meadowland. It was hoped that the elk would multiply, insuring the saving of the species, and eventually be released to wander freely in the park.

THE YOSEMITE ELK HERD

The California Valley Elk, Tule Elk, or Dwarf Elk was once extremely abundant in the lower valleys of California but probably never ranged into the mountains as far as Yosemite. The species has been so reduced in numbers that in recent years it has been in danger of extinction. A few of the animals were given refuge in Yosemite Valley where a small herd is maintained in a large paddock near Yosemite Village. It is to be hoped that ultimately a sufficiently large refuge will be established in either the San Joaquin or Sacramento Valley so that these animals can be transferred to their native habitat—the last survivors of a noble native big game mammal that is now in grave danger of being crowded by man from the face of the earth.

[70]

The Yosemite Elk Herd
YOSEMITE VALLEY - An Intimate Guide
By Ansel F. Hall, Chief Naturalist, National Park Service
Illustrated by Leo Zellensky
Copyright June 1929 by the National Park Publishing House, Berkeley, California

1923 photograph of Tule Elk in their paddock.
From author's collection.

By 1933, the herd had increased to twenty-seven in number. However, they were not a native species in the Yosemite area, the eight-foot high fence enclosing the paddock was not attractive and the elk were over-grazing the meadow in the enclosure. Other obvious problems were that park visitors would tromp across the unenclosed sections of meadow to get a closer look at the elk and take the opportunity to pet and feed the "wild" animals. For those reasons the elk were moved to the Owens Valley in Inyo County that same year.

Since the elk did not roam freely but were kept in a pen down-valley from the Ahwahnee Hotel near the "New" Yosemite Village and south of the museum, happening upon the pastoral scene in the Ahwahnee Hotel postcard would have been next to impossible.

I have no idea how the elk may have been placed so idyllically at ease in front of the Ahwahnee Hotel's patio area. Had someone herded or trucked them up to the hotel and then tethered them into position? How do you get two large animals that are used to wandering around relatively freely to both park themselves in the perfect spot for such a well composed photograph?

There is, of course, the possibility that the postcard had been somehow "doctored up".

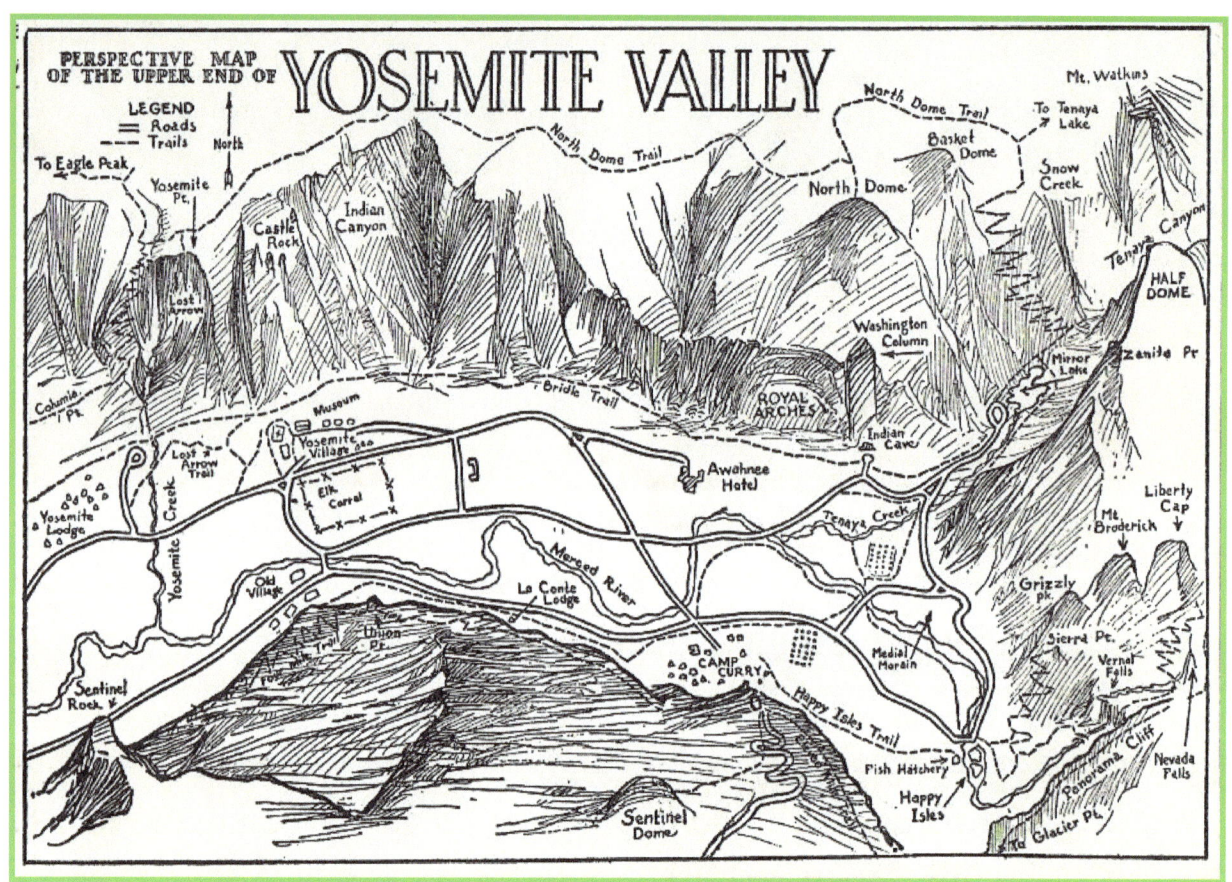

Perspective map showing the locations of both the 'Elk Corral' (left of center) and the Awahnee [sic] Hotel (right of center).
From *Yosemite Valley an Intimate Guide* [1929] by Ansel F. Hall, Chief Naturalist, National Park Service. Illustrated by Leo Zellensky. National Parks Publishing House, Berkeley, California.

Photograph with this citation written on back: "Herd of Elk (Cooling off in pool), Yosemite 6/24/32"
From author's collection.

Park visitors getting a close look at the Tule elk in their corral.
National Park Service Historic Photograph Collection.

Courtesy of the Yosemite National Park Research Library.

What's Wrong With This Picture? - Yosemite National Park

Photos from author's collection.

Postcards from author's collection.

Just one more item about the Tule elk in Yosemite Valley –

The two postcards on the preceding page were published by The Western Publishing & Novelty Co., Los Angeles, California and both have the ID/card number 348.

You will notice that the first postcard is a color tinted version of the card shown at the beginning of the discussion about the Tule elk on page 67. This card is classified as a "White Border Era" postcard and was published between the years 1915 to 1930 when the elk could have been seen in Yosemite Valley.

The second postcard is classified as a "Linen Era" postcard because of the linen fibers used in the card stock. This postcard was published roughly between the years 1930 to 1945.

Remember, the herd of Tule elk was removed from Yosemite Valley in 1933.

These color tinted postcards are almost identical except for one glaring item: the elk have miraculously disappeared from the later card!

Now you see them, now you don't.

Postcard - **Husbandry in the Midst of Grandeur, Yosemite Valley, Cal.**
No. Y. 27. Publ. by Newman Post Card Co., Los Angeles, Cal.
From author's collection

This is a simple yet beautiful postcard of a scene in Yosemite Valley. In my opinion, there are two things wrong with this postcard.

First of all, the best features of the scenery are hidden from view. Both Half Dome and the Royal Arches are almost completely hidden by tree branches. Secondly, the featured theme is "husbandry," which would be agriculture: the act or practice of cultivating crops and breeding and raising livestock. And yet there are no crops or livestock in the picture. I guess our imaginations are supposed to conclude that since there is a barbed wire fence with a gate depicted, there must be husbandry of some sort going on.

So, basically this is a pretty postcard showing a road, some fencing, trees and some mountain scenery.

Is there some way a simple scene such as this could have been improved upon?

Of course there is! Take a similar picture and paint in some bison grazing in the meadows!

Postcard - **Half Dome, Yosemite Valley**
AMERIC. HIST. ART. PUBL. CO. - New York, 111 East 14 Str.
Printed in Germany, K.V.G.G. Lange, B.L. Schwalbach. Y.V.S.B. 205
From author's collection.

And, hey, if it looks good on one postcard, why not add bison to another card as well?

Postcard – **El Capitan, Yosemite Valley**
AMERIC. HIST. ART. PUBL. CO. - New York, 111 East 14 Str.
Printed in Germany, K.V.G.G. Lange, B.L. Schwalbach. Y.V.S.b. 207
From author's collection

I think bison are extremely cool animals. They're huge, strong and impressive looking. That's probably why the National Park Service put an image of one on their emblem.

I even think that their scientific designation is cool. The genus is *Bison*; the American bison or buffalo is *Bison bison*; the two subspecies in the United States are *Bison bison bison* (Plains bison) and *Bison bison athabascae* (Wood bison).

However, there has not been a bison in Yosemite or anywhere nearby in recorded history. There aren't even any fossil records that I could find of there ever being bison in Yosemite. The closest a bison got to Yosemite was when his hide was traded by a tribe on the eastern slope of the Sierras and brought back to be used as a cloak or blanket.

The artist(s) and/or publisher of these postcards was either extremely confused about Yosemite wildlife or just went overboard with artistic license.

Unfortunately, however, the "husbandry" with the barbed wire fences and gates shown in the postcards where all too true. Plenty of cattle for meat and cows for dairy products were raised in the Valley. There were also fruit orchards, large gardens, fields plowed for crops and hay, and meadows used as grazing land.

Unlike today when fencing is used mainly to protect meadows and facilitate their restoration, land fenced in by barbed wire was everywhere in the Valley from the late 1850's until the National Park Service did what it could to keep land use to a minimum and in its natural state.

HALF DOME FROM THE ROADWAY: A Wonderful Picture – The Road Shaded by Pines and Firs. Ahead the Great Half Dome.
Published by Passenger Dep't Southern Pacific Company 1904, Southern Pacific Company – Sunset, Ogden & Shasta Routes
Engraved by Sunset Photo Engraving Co. Printed by Sunset Press, San Francisco

Barbed wire fences in Ahwahnee Meadow, circa 1920s.
Photo from author's collection.

And, as these pictures show, instead of bison grazing freely, there were plenty of beef and dairy cattle fenced in.

Fenced cattle in Yosemite Valley.
National Park Service Historic Photograph Collection.

Stereoview - **Yo Semite Falls, 2,634 feet high (Group of Spanish Cattle.), Yo Semite Valley, California.**
Yosemite Stereoviews by C.L. Pond - American Scenery number 683
The Bancroft Library. University of California, Berkeley.

Postcard, circa 1907 to 1915 – **Hotel Wawona, Yosemite Valley, California.**
Published by Edward H. Mitchell, San Francisco, Cal., #1431.
From author's collection.

Detail from postcard above.

The National Park Story in Pictures
By Isabelle F. Story, Consultant, National Park Service
UNITED STATES GOVERNMENT PRINTING OFFICE, *WASHINGTON: 1957*

DAIRY MILKING HEADQUARTERS, LEIDIG MEADOW, 1918, *Yosemite National Park.*
"In 1918, when the National Park Service was in its infancy, cattle used the meadows in Yosemite National Park and a dairy milking headquarters was maintained at the edge of Leidig Meadow in Yosemite Valley."
The National Park Story in Pictures by Isabelle F. Story, Consultant, National Park Service
UNITED STATES GOVERNMENT PRINTING OFFICE, *WASHINGTON: 1957*

Fortunately, Yosemite now has very few fenced in areas. I personally don't recall ever seeing a barbed wire fence in Yosemite; my first visit to the park was in 1959. I see plenty of mule deer and never any cattle. And over in Leidig Meadow, west of Yosemite Lodge (The Lodge at the Falls), you will no longer find a "dairy milking headquarters" covered with manure and muck stinking up the place.

At times I wonder about the image on the postcard and how cool it would be to see a small herd of bison grazing in one of the meadows; just once anyway.

PART TWO

GLACIER POINT – GETTING THERE AND SHOWING OFF

AN IMPORTANT CAUTIONARY NOTE:

IN THE FOLLOWING SECTION OF THIS BOOK ARE NUMEROUS PICTURES OF PEOPLE ENGAGING IN DANGEROUS AND SOMETIMES FOOLISH ACTIVITIES THAT COULD HAVE RESULTED IN SERIOUS INJURY OR EVEN DEATH TO THEMSELVES OR OTHERS. SUCH DEPICTIONS DO NOT IN ANY WAY CONDONE SUCH BEHAVIOR OR THE TAKING OF UNNECESSARY AND DANGEROUS RISKS.

Photo by Taber, S. F.
UP THE ZIGZAGS, NEAR NEVADA FALL.

"Up the Zigzags, Near Nevada Fall"

There are two routes by trail from Yosemite Valley to Glacier Point. One once referred to as the "Short Trail", or the Four Mile Trail, and a longer route that starts at Happy Isles via Vernal and Nevada Falls and the Panorama Trail.

(There was an even shorter "trail" of about 1.5 miles that ran from Camp Curry up the cliff face to Glacier Point. It was so steep that it was more of a climb than a hike. It was so notoriously steep and dangerous that it was strongly advised that one only go up the trail but not return by the same route.)

On the "Long Trail", about 11 miles, a section of steep switchbacks that leads to the top of Nevada Falls was known as The Zigzags or Zig Zags.

I found the preceding photograph in the *Yosemite Souvenir & Guide* by D. J. Foley, 1902 (second year) edition.

Daniel J. Foley was a photographer who opened a photographic studio and print shop known as the Yosemite Tourist Printing Office and Studio, or "Tourist" Studio, circa 1891. Here he took photos of visitors, sold postcards, published and sold a souvenir paper called 'The Yosemite Tourist' and beginning in 1901 started publishing the *Yosemite Souvenir & Guide*.

The photograph on the preceding page is credited to "Taber, S.F.". Isaiah West Taber was the owner of a well known photographic studio in San Francisco which he operated from 1871 until 1906, when the great earthquake occurred. However, Taber may not have been the photographer of this picture as he printed, published, and distributed the work of other photographers, including Carleton Watkins.

I found it amusing that while the caption is "Up the Zigzags, Near Nevada Fall" no one seems to have noticed at the time of publication that the horses and riders are all headed ***down hill***.

There were many similar photos and postcards available at the time showing riders actually going ***up*** the trail, like the next item . . .

Postcard - "The Zig Zag Trail, Yosemite"
Made by a New Patented Process by Pillsbury's Pictures, Inc.
Yosemite National Park, Cal.
From author's collection.

This postcard was published by Arthur C. Pillsbury. He was a photographer, inventor, naturalist and over-all quite innovative gentleman.

His Pillsbury Picture Company of Oakland, California, purchased the Studio of the Three Arrows in Yosemite Valley in about 1907. He ran this photo studio until 1928 when he sold out to the Yosemite Park and Curry Company.

I could find nothing definitive but this postcard seems to be circa 1915. (see previous page) When marketed in a color tinted lithograph edition it was catalogued as No. Y136 "The Zig Zag Trail, Yosemite Valley, Cal."

I include this picture to demonstrate that congested traffic conditions in Yosemite during the peak tourist season are nothing new. There are at least thirty-six riders on horses and mules shown on this small section of trail on the way to the top of Nevada Fall. How many others may have been out-of-frame is anyone's guess.

Postcard photo #440 by George Fiske. No Caption.
Views of Yosemite by George Fiske, Identifier: 58
The Bancroft Library. University of California, Berkeley.

This third postcard of the Zig Zag Trail was taken by George Fiske. Mr. Fiske first came to Yosemite Valley in 1872 spending the summers in Yosemite and the winters in San Francisco. He opened a photographic studio in the "Lower Village" in 1879 and lived in the Valley year-round.

When Mr. Fiske took his photo, he apparently was on the trail on a slow day. Unlike A. C. Pillsbury's postcard, there are only two horses and one lone man on the Zig Zag Trail.

It might have been the time of year or just the time of day, but George had the trail pretty much to himself. Mr. Pillsbury seemed to have gotten stuck in rush hour traffic.

Some things never change.

The following picture and text is an excerpt from the <u>YOSEMITE Souvenir and Guide</u> by D. J. Foley, second edition, "Tourist" Studio, Yosemite, Cal., May I, 1902.

"Oh Papa I'se joying my self"
Photo by [George] Fiske, Yosemite
Courtesy Yosemite Research Library

"PLUM DUFF"

The above picture represents how Dorothy and Ned Atkinson, whose home is in the Valley, came down the zigzag trail from Glacier Point. The latter is 3,250 feet above the floor of the Valley. The trail is four miles long. Into the bag on the left Ned was carefully tucked away and tied in, for he had the danger side, because from many turns on the way he could look down a thousand feet or more. "Plum Duff," too, seemed to delight in getting as close as possible to the outer edges of the dangerous turns. His sister was put into the opposite bag, and thus safely loaded, with Mrs. Atkinson leading the faithful animal, they rode down to their Valley home.

This picture would have been taken when Yosemite Valley was still administered by the State of California and Yosemite National Park surrounded the Valley.

This was also when the Four Mile Trail was actually four miles long, as opposed to the 4.6 or 4.8 (depending on the source) miles it is today. It is one of the steepest trails in the Yosemite Valley area. Before the trail was rerouted in the 1920's, which made it longer, there were sections of trail that were actually steeper.

If you have ever hiked the Four Mile Trail yourself, you know what I am talking about. Many that know how steep the trail is choose to only hike it either up or down, not both. They hike one way and pay to ride the park shuttle service the other. Even then, it's so steep it takes a toll on your legs either way you choose to go.

The children's mother, Nell Atkinson, was kind enough to tie Ned into the bag he was stuffed into because, after all, he rode down on the "danger side" of the trail, the side with all the best views.

Even though burros, like little Plum Duff, are extremely sure footed animals, it had to be one heart pounding experience. Can you imagine being a little kid like Ned hanging out over the edge of the cliffs when "'Plum Duff,' too, seemed to delight in getting as close as possible to the outer edges of the dangerous turns"?

I wonder how often this harrowing trip was made.

I'm sure that both Ned and his sister Dorothy were glad when they were big enough to walk up and down the trail on their own power instead of being lugged around by a burro like a piece of luggage.

Stereoview from author's collection.

This photo from a stereoview is captioned: "Yosemite Falls from Glacier Point Trail, California, U. S. A.", is copyrighted 1894 by Strohmeyer & Wyman and was sold by Underwood & Underwood.

The riders are going up the "Short Trail" or the "Four Mile Trail" to Glacier Point.

The horse in the lead is white, being ridden by a woman sitting sidesaddle, legs on the left of her mount. She is wearing a flat brimmed hat with her hair worn up; a dress with dark, puffy shoulders and long sleeves.

The second horse is white and is being ridden by a man wearing a dark cap, dark jacket and pants and knee-high boots. There is another white horse or mule following just behind.

Stereoview from author's collection.

This photo from a stereoview is captioned: "Yosemite Falls from Glacier Point Trail, California, U. S. A.", is copyrighted 1899 by Strohmeyer & Wyman and was sold by Underwood & Underwood.

The riders are going down the "Short Trail" or the "Four Mile Trail" from Glacier Point.

The horse in the lead is white, being ridden by a woman sitting sidesaddle, legs on the left of her mount. She is wearing a flat brimmed hat with her hair worn up; a dress with dark, puffy shoulders and long sleeves.

The second horse is also white, being ridden by a man wearing a dark cap, dark jacket and pants and knee-high boots. There is a man in a wide brimmed hat on a white horse or mule following just behind.

There's something awfully familiar about these two stereoviews!

The same people wearing the same clothes on the same trail, in fact in the same spot on the trail? (Look at the detail of the rocks in the foreground of each picture.) The same copyright owner and both stereoviews sold by Underwood & Underwood.

So, it would seem that these tourists rode up to Glacier Point in 1894 and didn't come back down until 1899 and decided to wear the same clothes. They must have only had one set of riding togs.

Or, more likely, they had their picture taken on the same day at the same spot; both on the way up and then back down. I wonder if they went all the way to the top first or did a U-turn somewhere on the trail to save the trouble of the cameraman of either waiting around or having to set up the equipment twice.

I'm just trying to figure out the necessity of showing the same riders going up the trail and then back down. Was it to alleviate some irrational fear that you could go up but couldn't get back down by the same route?

Of course there's the chance it was just a way of selling stereoviews to people thinking they had a newer set of views in 1899 than they had in 1894.

But wait! There's more!

It just doesn't seem that Underwood & Underwood could get enough shots of certain scenes and subjects. This is true of riders on horses on the trail to Glacier Point with Yosemite Falls in the background taken at the *same* location.

Here's just one more from the Library of Congress Prints and Photographs Online Catalog (PPOC), copyright 1901.

Guess what the caption is!

"Yosemite Falls, from Glacier Point Trail, Yosemite Valley, California."

Library of Congress Prints and Photographs Division
Reproduction Number: LC-USZ62-97305, Digital ID: cph 3b43406, Control #89711583
Copyright 1901 by Underwood & Underwood

Photo from author's collection.

With a sign posted for years about the "difference between bravery and just plain ordinary foolishness" in an attempt to persuade people up on Glacier Point not to take unnecessary chances for a better view, a cheap thrill and/or a photo opportunity one would think that the danger would be taken more seriously.

There was also this postcard sold as a souvenir or to send friends to show how high above Yosemite Valley you had been when up at Glacier Point. (Not just 3,000 feet but 3,254 feet up to be exact.)

Postcard from author's collection.

I'm not sure when the sign was posted, but I had another photograph of it dated August 1921. The postcard above was sold beginning in about 1930. But, before the sign was posted and afterwards, how dangerous the cliff was didn't seem to matter to anybody. With or without a sign, people were going to go out on one of the two rock masses projecting out over Yosemite Valley, the Overhanging Rock and Photographers Rock, anyway.

The following are just a few of the many thousands and thousands of published and private photographs taken over the years of people having a little bit of fun or just plain showing off. Getting your picture taken while you were out hanging over the thin air was the thing to do.

Some showed a little bit of timidity –

James D. Phelan Photograph Albums, Volume 85 Identifier: 230
The Bancroft Library. University of California, Berkeley.

OVER HANGING ROCK 3,234 feet above valley floor.
Photo by Boysen Studio Yosemite, Cal.
From *YOSEMITE VALLEY ROMANCE* by William Lee Popham, 1911

Postcard from author's collection.

Photos from author's collection.

Some posed grandly, either alone or in groups –

Stereoview - **Nearly a mile straight down and only a step— from Glacier Point (N.W.) across valley to Yosemite Falls.**
Underwood & Underwood, publishers, c1902.
Library of Congress Prints and Photographs Division.

Overhanging Rock, Glacier Point
Copyright, 1901, by H. G. (Henry Greenwood) Peabody, Boston.
Library of Congress Prints and Photographs Division.

On Glacier Rock, Yosemite (3,200 feet from the ground below), California, U.S.A.
Strohmeyer & Wyman Identifier: 16084, 1894
Zelda Mackay Collection of Stereographic Views,
The Bancroft Library. University of California, Berkeley.

View from Glacier Point
Taber Photo, San Francisco, #B1003
Miscellaneous California and Mexico Views,
The Bancroft Library. University of California, Berkeley.

From *Motoring Thru the Yosemite* by H. B. Magill
Yosemite Publishing Co., 111 Seventh Street, San Francisco, California
Copyright 1923 by H. B. Magill

Some persons tried to look relaxed and nonchalant –

Postcard - Overhanging Rock, Glacier Point
Pillsbury Picture Co., Nº 45
From author's collection.

Nearly a mile straight down and only a step, Yosemite from Glacier Point, Cal.
Strohmeyer & Wyman #47, 1894.
Zelda Mackay Collection of Stereographic Views, Identifier: 16085
The Bancroft Library. University of California, Berkeley.

Over hanging rock on Yosemite Falls, from Glacier
James D. Phelan Photograph Albums, Volume 94. Identifier: 55
The Bancroft Library. University of California, Berkeley.

From author's collection.

From author's collection.

From author's collection.

And some looked like they were really enjoying themselves –

Stereoview – **Overlooking Nature's grandest scenery – from Glacier Point (N.E.), Yosemite Valley, Cal.**
Keystone View Company, #6031/15. Copyrighted, Underwood & Underwood
From author's collection.

Photo from author's collection.

Stereoview - **Glacier Point, Yosemite Valley, Cal.** Geo. W. Griffith, c1902.
Library of Congress Prints and Photographs Division.

Detail from Private Mailing Card
**Sadie Young on the Overhanging Rock 3200 ft.
Above the Floor of the Yosemite Valley . . . . .**
Postmarked July, 1903
From author's collection.

Detail from Private Mailing Card
Postmarked May, 1902.
Probably Kitty Tatch.
From author's collection.

"Kitty Tatch and her friend Katherine Hazelton on overhanging rock."
George Fiske, circa 1900
National Park Service Historic Photograph Collection.
Catalog Number: HPC-001067

There reached a point when the National Park Service felt it would be best to place a barrier of some sort along the ledges of Glacier Point to help prevent accidents from occurring. It's amazing that, for some reason, there never were any fatal accidents from people falling off the top of the cliff, with or without barriers, until 2006.

"World Famous Viewpoint – Glacier Point"
Released by Publicity Department, Yosemite Park & Curry Co., Yosemite National Park
April 1, 1942
Photo from author's collection.

Here are some photos of the railing type barriers that were installed as they looked in the 1950's or 60's. They certainly look safe. And while the rails are high enough to discourage anyone from climbing over for any reason, they are also close enough to the edge that one can still get excellent views of Yosemite Valley, even straight down to Curry Village (previously Camp Curry).

This looks like a nice unobstructed view. And this woman would certainly not be able to get any closer to the edge of the cliff, unless she climbed over the barrier.

Photo from author's collection.

And the man in the next shot is certainly as close to the edge as most anybody would want to get. The bottom photo shows where the fir bark was stacked and set ablaze every day so that in the evening the still glowing embers could be pushed off to create the nightly Firefall (or Fire Fall). [I'll get to that soon enough.]

Photos from author's collection.

However, from the next photographs, you can see that it just didn't matter. People still went over or through the barriers to get that photograph that had become so famous over the years. (And unfortunately, they still do.)

Photo from author's collection.

Notice the railing on the left hand side in this photo. Apparently a lot of people will always feel that the obvious meaning of the barriers is meant for others, not themselves. This person obviously felt that they were an exception and that getting themselves photographed out on Overhanging Rock was more important than personal safety, or setting the proper example for everyone else.

Photo from author's collection.

Judging from the bend in the top rung of this railing, there must be some awfully heavy people leaning or climbing over it.

You can see the barrier in the photo below in the upper right corner.

Photo from author's collection.

OVERHANGING ROCK, GLACIER POINT
3,250 feet
Galen Clark standing on Overhanging Rock
Photo by George Fiske
From *The Yosemite Valley* by Galen Clark (1910)

The information concerning the previous photograph is that George Fiske took it circa 1900. That would mean that the subject in the picture, Galen Clark, was eighty-five or eighty-six years old at the time.

It's not that Mr. Clark was some sickly, feeble old man at the time. He could really get around and was quite active for a man of his age. He died just before his ninety-sixth birthday in 1910. That's quite an achievement for a man that came to the Sierra Nevada Mountains in 1856 at the age of forty-two ailing with tuberculosis and given a 50/50 chance of living six months.

Even though there were so many hundreds of photographs published of people standing out on Overhanging Rock, I can't recall more than a few that were taken in the winter, let alone an elderly gentleman in the scene.

And here we have eighty-five year old Galen Clark out on this snow covered icy rock ledge to have his picture taken. Even if he was a much younger man, the thought of him sliding right off the edge is scary. I mean, look at the size of those icicles! That had to be some nice, slick ice he was standing on.

Winter! Ice and snow! Not safe!

But, hey, it's Galen Clark. He'd been doing this kind of thing for most of his life. John Muir, quite the agile climber and scrambler himself, had this to say about his friend: "Galen Clark was the best mountaineer I ever met."

It was just another day in the life of "Mr. Yosemite."

Postcard - **"Winkey" at Glacier Point**
From author's collection.

This postcard was produced by Arthur C. Pillsbury, a well known photographer of Yosemite scenery and producer of numerous postcards for sale to tourists visiting the national park.

When everyone and their aunt was publishing and selling pictures, postcards and stereoviews of the same subjects, sometimes something a bit different and novel was needed to increase sales.

One of the most popular topics for pictures sold to tourists was of people sitting, standing or doing other activities on the Overhanging Rock at Glacier Point. Something a little more gimmicky would sell better.

This postcard is catalogued as P.P. (Pillsbury's Pictures) No. 1037. The brave animal seen here out on Overhanging Rock was Mr. Pillsbury's personal beast of burden, his donkey "Winkey".

I always wonder when I look at this card how Winkey was cajoled into walking out onto the ledge and what it took to make him stay there long enough for the picture to be taken. It's sort of sad and amusing at the same time.

It's even sadder to realize that Winkey most likely carried all the photographic and other equipment up and back down the trail for the picture to be taken. Now that's exploitation!

The concept worked well, though. I bought the postcard, close to a hundred years after it was printed, and even had it framed.

Postcard - "A Tumbler of Marvelous Nerve on Overhanging Rock"
Boysen Studio, Yosemite National Park, California
From author's collection

The original picture on this postcard was taken by Julius T. Boysen circa 1903. Mr. Boysen came to Yosemite Valley about 1898 and originally operated his photography business out of a tent in the Old Yosemite Village. In 1900 when the Yosemite Commissioners decided that there should be no tents allowed on the main road of the village he built a small studio.

The postcard was originally sold as a color lithograph with the caption shown below this card. A similar postcard I once had, postmarked 1911, had the caption "Overhanging Rock at Glacier Point, 3200 feet from the floor of the Valley, Yosemite, Cal." - just in case one wanted to know how far this person would fall if he lost his balance.

Some years later, real photo postcards in black and white or sepia tones became popular, so this postcard was re-released as seen here without any caption. This postcard would have been sold circa 1925.

I don't know why this gymnast did what he did, but it sure makes for an interesting picture. It appears that a small platform was built and placed on the rock for him do to this stunt. Did that somehow make it safer to do?

Anyway, doing something a little different with a familiar topic, taking unnecessary, dangerous risks in front of a camera, helped sell postcards.

"Balanced on His Head"
Library of Congress Prints and Photographs Division

Here is another photo by J. T. Boysen, taken circa 1902. I found this one on file in the Library of Congress archives. It is listed only as a photographic print. I don't know if it ever appeared in any book of the period or was published in any way.

Apparently there was no shortage of daredevils visiting Yosemite willing to risk their necks to have themselves immortalized doing something extremely dangerous, albeit anonymously.

Photograph courtesy of Hank Johnston.

Yet another photo by J. T. Boysen, but this time we know who the daredevil is. This is Antonio Gillette risking life and limb for the camera and fleeting fame.

Photographer anonymous.
Photograph courtesy of Ted Orland
© Ted Orland.

"What fools these mortals be!" indeed; the emphasis being on the word "fools".

Photo from author's collection.

You just have to wonder - what does it prove and was it worth it?

Oliver Lippincott driving his Locomobile in Yosemite Valley.
National Park Service Historic Photograph Collection.

On June 23, 1900, the first automobile to enter a National Park was driven into Yosemite.*

Oliver Lippincott, the owner of the auto, was accompanied by Edward Russell, who was hired as driver/mechanic. The car was made by the Locomobile Company of Bridgeport, Connecticut.

*Many sources state that the date this occurred was June 24, 1900. However in the book *Ho! For Yo-Semite* by Hank Johnston, copyright ©2000 by the Yosemite Association, Mr. Johnston points out that Oliver Lippincott registered at the Sentinel Hotel in Yosemite Valley on the night of June 23.

It was a steam powered vehicle with two cylinders that produced ten horsepower and had a top speed of 40 miles per hour. Lippincott and Russell spent more than two weeks in Yosemite, where Lippincott hoped to promote Yosemite as a vacation locale (he was a photographer by trade and set up a photography shop in Yosemite Valley the next year) as well as promote the Locomobile Company.

Being the driver of the first automobile into Yosemite was history making, but that is not where the novelty of this trip ended.

After the superintendent of the Yosemite Stage & Turnpike Company, Henry Washburn, was given an eight mile ride around the valley in the little auto, he persuaded Edward Russell to drive the auto up to Glacier Point. This would mean a drive up steep, winding stage roads and a rise in elevation of over 3200 feet (Lippincott made the trip following the car in a horse-drawn carriage). The little car made the trip from the valley to the Mountain House Hotel on Glacier Point in five hours.

Oliver Lippincott, a Los Angeles photographer, posed on Glacier Point, Yosemite.
National Park Service Historic Photograph Collection.

The next morning Mr. Lippincott decided that his Locomobile must somehow be gotten out onto the famous Overhanging Rock for a photograph or two. This would certainly be a great promotion for the car company. But it was no small task.

(I honestly have no idea where I got this picture, but I'm going to use it anyway.)

One of the pictures taken on that occasion appeared the next year in a magazine advertisement for the Locomobile Company of America. The text is a little misleading.

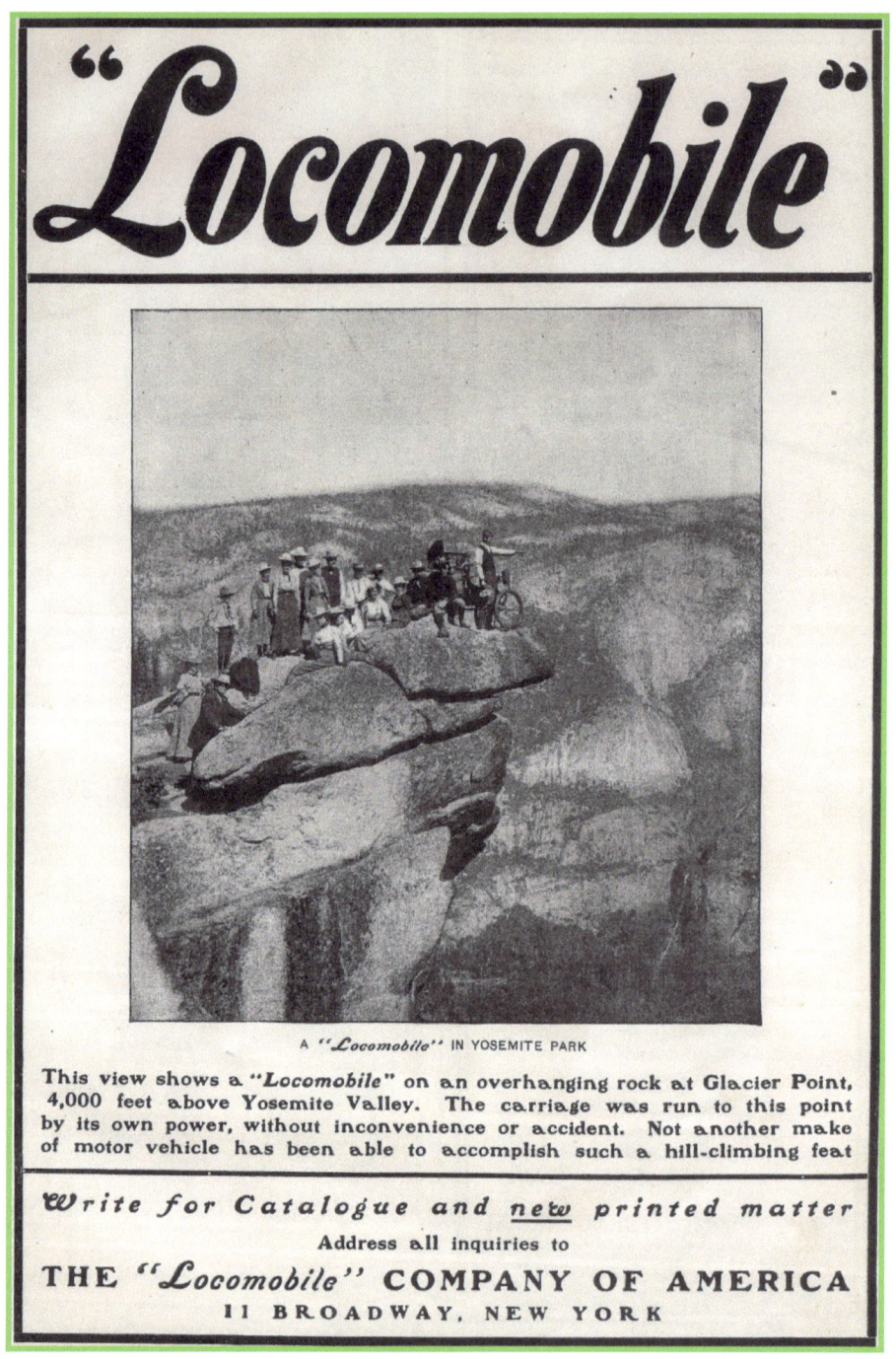

1901 magazine advertisement.
From author's collection.

The ad states that "The carriage was run to this point by its own power, without inconvenience or accident." Oliver Lippincott gave quite a different account of how his car was "posed" for its picture. His side of the story is found in the book *Ho! For Yo-Semite* by Hank Johnston:

Nothing would do the next morning but that the locomobile must go out on the overhanging rock where only the most fearless and level-headed have ever dared to stand. The little machine was rolled out to the point, and then everyone paused, looking at the machine and then at the rock. The general opinion was that it could not be done.

A. H. Washburn said nothing, but mounted the rock himself with a firm step and took observations, then, turning to the crowd, said from his elevated position:

"Now, I'm going to show you that it can be done, too."

He ordered one of the guides to bring him two stout ropes and some logs of wood; then called to his assistance the stout arms and trained muscles of "Babe" Burnett, Stanford's next year football captain, who was one of the Automobile party. Together with the other men of the party they succeeded in dragging the locomobile, only weighing 650 pounds, over the mound of rocks nearer and nearer the edge of the cliff. The women assembled on the rocks and buried their heads in their hands, horrified at the sight. I remember looking up once. There was the overhanging rock, which is fairly suspended above the valley, excepting for one little corner, while below yawned an abyss of over 3500 feet. At the very edge of this stood the reckless guide, Walter Henesley, with one of his heels projecting over the valley, tugging away at the locomobile, which was inclined at such an angle that it seemed ready to roll over at any moment. Two inches less space and it would have gone plunging down into the valley. On the other side, Washburn and Burnett, both with ropes tied about their waists, sure to go with it if it should start; while others were lifting or bracing it in equally perilous positions. I firmly believe that if the machine had gone over every man of the party would have gone with it. At last it was out in a firm position, and we grouped ourselves around it, fairly hanging on with tooth and nail while the camera was adjusted. No picture was ever so long in being taken. I was sure I felt the rock shaking under me.

So, when the ad stated that "the carriage was run to this point by its own power, without inconvenience", that was more than just a little stretch of the truth. Looking at the photographs, I don't think Mr. Lippincott was exaggerating.

As for the statement "Not another make of motor vehicle has been able to accomplish such a hill-climbing feat," that was true, seeing as this was the first automobile to ever have been there. That was just a matter of semantics.

This was one of the most dangerous stunts ever pulled for the benefit of the camera on Overhanging Rock.

But then . . .

Postcard from the collection of Ed Herny.

If Oliver Lippincott could get his little Locomobile out on Overhanging Rock why couldn't someone else do it again; and in a bigger and better way?

That's what photographer Arthur C. Pillsbury decided to do in 1916. The how's and why's is explained in an article from the San Francisco Bay Area Post Card Club newsletter of February 2004 –

> Arthur Pillsbury never forgot the photo of the Locomobile on Overhanging Rock, and ultimately decided he would stage a similar exhibition for his own camera. On June 10, 1916 Pillsbury broke the driving time record from Oakland to Yosemite in his new Studebaker Six, covering the distance via Big Oak Flat Road in less than nine hours. Three months later, to prove he could pass yet another difficult test, he navigated the Studebaker up to Glacier Point on a sunny mid-September morning. Surveying the approach to Overhanging Rock it was determined that a runway was necessary to pass over several boulders that barred the way. Carpenters working on the Desmond Glacier Point Hotel quickly agreed to erect a trestle, and the car was slowly edged outward. The rock measures roughly seven feet wide and fourteen feet long, and beneath falls blue space for 3240 feet. The driver stopped about a foot from the rock's edge. Pillsbury's photo postcard recording the event shows Foster Curry at the wheel and Arthur Pillsbury himself straddling the hood. Pennants reading "Yosemite" and "Studebaker 1916" are attached to the car. Facial expressions on the fourteen people around and in the automobile betray some degree of tension; but seven raised arms, some holding hats, succeed in giving a wave. Two of the men appear to be the helpful carpenters.
>
> San Francisco Bay Area Post Card Club Newsletter
> February 2004, Volume XIX, No. 2
> Article – *Where Only the Fearless Dare to Stand – Yosemite's Overhanging Rock* by Frank A. Sternad

When Oliver Lippincott had his little stunt photographed there were the small car (it weighed 650 pounds) and six people out actually on the rock. Arthur Pillsbury got a much bigger car and fourteen people out there! The Studebaker Six was fourteen feet six inches long and five feet 8 inches wide overall. It **barely** fit out on that rock. And it had a gross weight of 2,925 pounds.* If you add in the fourteen people at an average weight of 150 pounds each, that's another 2,100 pounds. That was an awful lot of mass hanging out there in space.

*History of the Studebaker Corporation by Albert Russel Erskine.
Chicago, The Studebaker Corporation, 1924.

Postcard from the collection of Ed Herny.

Just how precarious getting the Studebaker out onto the Overhanging Rock was can be seen in the preceding postcard. There are the carpenters on the ramp and platform they built to drive the car out onto the rock. You can see some rope or cable attached to the rear axle to keep the car from going over the edge.

An even closer look will show just how big a risk was being taken by these men to position the car before the big group photo was taken. This was really sticking your neck out. Take a look at the man positioned by the front wheel. I don't know what he was doing but there is no room for error – literally. That front tire is on the very edge and he has somehow found enough room to squat down and tinker around.

What a way to get a photograph!

When you are looking at the various pictures of anywhere from a single individual to groups of people, all the way up to automobiles perched on the Overhanging Rock on Glacier Point, it would be good to have an idea of how extremely dangerous it really was.

Again, for many years this sign was posted as a means to dissuade people from taking unnecessary chances on the edge of a cliff that, if one was to fall off, it would be at least a good 1500 feet or farther before the first bounce.

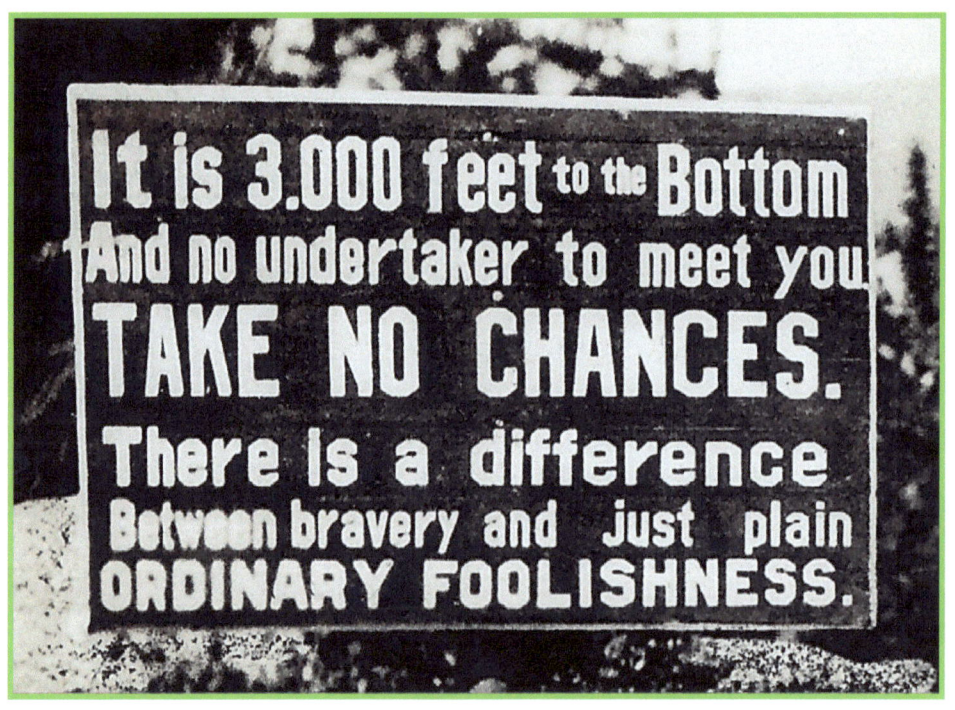

From author's collection.

The following two photographs give a very good perspective of how far the fall from the top would be.

Look closely at both of them and in each you will see a small speck on the top of Glacier Point on the rock that juts out. That small speck is a man standing on the edge. You might need a loupe or magnifying glass to see him. The rest is just cliff and air, with Half Dome in the background.

The first photo is attributed to Carleton Watkins taken in the 1860's showing a mere speck of a person on the Overhanging Rock. (Look *real* hard!)

"Glacier Point and Half Dome from trail. Yosemite Valley, Cal."
Photographer Carleton E. Watkins, 186-?
Publisher I. W. (Isaiah West) Taber, printed between 1877 and 1890?
Caption printed in negative by I.W. Taber: "Taber number 1019." Attribution to Watkins is in doubt.
The Bancroft Library, University of California, Berkeley

This next photo was taken by Arthur Pillsbury circa 1914 showing a man on "Photographers Rock," a second rock slab that jutted out into thin air.

Silhouette profile of the cliff at Glacier Point, Yosemite National Park, California.
The man at the top stands on Photographers Rock, the smaller of the two overhanging slabs at the edge of the great precipice. Half Dome in the background.
Photo by A.C. Pillsbury, circa 1914.
Plate 20-B, U.S. Geological Survey Professional paper 160.

Having presented how far one would drop if one were to accidently fall off the top of Glacier Point and shown just a sample of the hundreds and thousands of pictures of those who have taken the risk to go out on the ledge, here is an incredible fact: According to the best records available, *only one person has ever accidently fallen to their death from the rim of Glacier Point*.

In the book Off the Wall: Death in Yosemite by Michael P. Ghiglieri and Charles R. "Butch" Farabee, Jr.*, every person that has died an unnatural death in Yosemite from when white Europeans first came upon the scene in 1851 until 2006 is recorded.

In chapter seven "Freak Accidents & Errors" is the sad account of Evan Anderson, age 20 –

> May 26, 2006 Glacier Point
>
> While standing at the safety railing at the Overlook, Anderson of Capitola, California dropped his digital camera over the edge. It landed on a ledge about 15 feet down. He leaned or climbed over the railing to assess retrieving his camera but fell 1,600 feet. Witnesses saw him fall in a spread-eagle, almost skydiving position which led investigators to suspect suicide. His lost camera became the clue convincing investigators it had been a freak accident.

I don't know how to explain how it is that only one person out of the thousands taking unnecessary risks has fallen from the top. But it certainly doesn't mean that it was ever a safe thing to do. And I know some people still sneak out on Overhanging Rock for the thrill and a quick photo to prove it. I've seen the pictures on the internet.

Don't do it!

*Copyright ©2007 by Michael P. Ghiglieri and Charles R. "Butch" Farabee, Jr., Puma Press, Flagstaff, Arizona.

PART 3

MISPLACED AND MISIDENTIFIED FEATURES

Postcard - **"Big Fall, Yosemite Valley, Cal."**
Illustrated Postal Card Co., New-York. Made in Germany.
From authors' collection.

Private Mailing Card - **"Big Fall, Yosemite Valley, Cal."**
Published 1898 by Arthur Livingston, Originator, N.Y.
From authors' collection.

The postcard on the previous page and this postcard both depict what is identified as being "Big Fall", supposedly in Yosemite Valley.

Although this waterfall may look similar to Upper Yosemite Fall, or even Bridal Veil or Ribbon Falls, there is no "Big Fall" in Yosemite National Park.

I suppose that if a publisher would like to sell picture postcards of waterfalls (and one waterfall looks pretty much like another) it helps sales if the fall is identified as being in a world famous locale. While the first postcard was made in Germany, both were distributed by publishers in the United States and both were available soon after the Spanish-American War in 1898.

The waterfall, however, is only misidentified.

The waterfall is correctly identified on another postcard by another publisher, shown here, published at about the same time. It is really Multnomah Falls which is east of Portland, Oregon and can be visited in what is now the Columbia River Gorge National Scenic Area.

Postcard - **Multnomah Falls**
No. 11 (23) - Frank S. Thayer, Publisher, Denver.
From author's collection.

Stereoview - **"Yosemite Valley, California"**
From author's collection.

This picture is one half of a lithographed stereoview of a waterfall identified as somehow being connected to Yosemite Valley. There is no printed information other than the caption on the card, not even the printer or publisher. This must have come from one of the most ambiguous sets of stereoviews ever sold. It's not even numbered so as to refer to a reference sheet for a fuller explanation of the view.

While this may look fairly similar to Vernal Fall in Yosemite, it's another waterfall that is found somewhere else in the United States. It is in the other National Park that begins with the letter 'Y' – Yellowstone.

This stereoview actually depicts the Lower Falls on the Yellowstone River in the Grand Canyon of the Yellowstone. It was also, on old postcards, stereoviews and photographs, often referred to as the "Grand Falls" or "Great Falls" of the Yellowstone River.

The photograph below is the Lower Falls of the Yellowstone River taken many years later from nearly the same perspective as the misidentified stereoview. If you ignore the rest of the scenery, it does look like Vernal Fall.

Lower falls of the Yellowstone River, Yellowstone National Park, circa 1936.
Photographer: John Hansen.
National Park Service Historic Photograph Collection.

Postcard - **"YOSEMITE FALLS, YOSEMITE VALLEY, CALIFORNIA"**
From author's collection.

While this postcard obviously is not showing Yosemite Falls, the descriptive information on the back of the card tells us this:

YOSEMITE FALLS, YOSEMITE VALLEY, CALIFORNIA
Over the precipices or bluffs rising perpendicularly 3000 ft. above the valley, are waterfalls pouring over its sides breaking into several laps. Many of them are known for their height and beauty, but the most picturesque and largest of all are the Yosemite, which drop unbroken for about half a mile, coming down with such torrent and roar attracting the attention of visitors for miles.

I really get a good laugh from this one.

This is actually another natural feature that is found in Yellowstone National Park. This is part of the Mammoth Hot Springs and is most likely the section known as the Jupiter Terrace.

I wonder where someone would have purchased this postcard originally. Was it sold in both Yellowstone and Yosemite? Hopefully, visitors to either park would have known that the description was wrong and would have bought it as a gag.

Postcard - **Three Sisters, Yosemite Valley.**
Publisher unknown, circa 1907 to 1915
From author's collection.

The caption on the back of this postcard reads:

> **Three Sisters, Yosemite Valley. –**
> The Three Sisters, Yosemite Valley, California, is one of the most beautiful natural wonders of this celebrated spot. No where on earth is there such a variety of natural beauty in cliffs, mountains, valleys, etc. as in the Yosemite Valley. A trail leads all around these Three Sisters, and the view of the surrounding valley from the trail as it winds in and out, is most enchanting.

There is a rock formation in Yosemite known as The Three **Brothers** on the north rim of Yosemite Valley between El Capitan and Yosemite Falls. The set of rock precipices that rise on the north of Bridal Veil Fall was once commonly called The Three **Graces** and is now identified "officially" as Cathedral Rocks. But there are no "Three Sisters" in Yosemite.

The Three Brothers, Height: 3,813 Feet
Photo by D. J. Foley
From *Yosemite the Beautiful*, circa 1905
D. J. Foley Publisher, "The Tourist Office", Yosemite, California
Bolte & Braden Company, San Francisco, California

The Three Graces and Leaning Tower
Photo by D. J. Foley
From *Yosemite the Beautiful*, circa 1905
D. J. Foley Publisher, "The Tourist Office", Yosemite, California
Bolte & Braden Company, San Francisco, California

The mountains shown on the postcard on page 158 are known as the "Three Sisters", but they are in the Canadian Rockies near Canmore, Alberta. They are known individually as Big Sister (Faith), Middle Sister (Charity) and Little Sister (Hope).

Postcard – **Three Sisters, Banff**
Made in Canada
Along the line of the Canadian Pacific Railway
Photographed and copyright by Byron Harmon, Banff, Canada
From author's collection.

Here are the real Three Sisters again, correctly identified, only without the strange purple and blue coloring that was on the first postcard.

I'm still confused about the "trail [that] leads all around" the Three Sisters, "and the view of the surrounding valley from the trail as it winds in and out". That must be one really long trail! And don't mountains usually surround a valley? I can't remember ever hearing of a valley surrounding the mountains before.

Stereoview - **"Upper Falls, Reflected in Lake Yosemite, Cal."**
Copyright 1898, by T. W. Ingersoll. Ingersoll View Company, St. Paul, Minn. U.S.A.
From author's collection.

One of the favorite subjects of photographers in Yosemite over the years has been to capture something being reflected in still waters. Mirror Lake is, of course, the best example of these scenes and there are numerous pictures of other locales.

Here is just one 19th century example of nature providing a double image of Upper Yosemite Falls for the camera to capture. The problem is that the reflection is said to be seen in "Lake Yosemite".

There is no "Lake Yosemite" in Yosemite National Park.

This picture is simply an example of just about any body of water having reflective properties when the surface is calm and the light is right. In this case it's the Merced River at high-water or in flood stage. Unless there has been very little snowfall during the winter in the mountains surrounding Yosemite Valley, there is going to be high water in the Merced River in the spring. The river will be deeper, wider and in many places in the valley, calmer, creating photo opportunities like this. (Heck, even I've been able to get pictures like that.)

"Lower Falls Reflected in 'Lake Yosemite', Cal."
Photo by author.
© 2012, Scott N. Tipton

Photographs such as these always seem to have something special about them. It seems to add more grandeur to something that is already spectacular. One of my favorite pictures with this theme was taken by Arthur C. Pillsbury, circa 1906.

"Yosemite Falls in Reflection"
Copyright by Pillsbury Picture Company. No. 142
Library of Congress Prints and Photographs Division Washington, D.C. 20540
Reproduction Number: LC-USZ62-124606, Digital ID: cph 3c24606, Control #: 00651056

I suppose that to have Yosemite Falls reflected in "Lake Yosemite" does make a more romantic caption than "the Merced River at Flood Stage." There's a less dangerous feel to it as well.

In fact, the Merced can get rather high in the spring, even in a normal year. The photo below was copyrighted in 1902, a year in which there was no recorded notable flooding. This picture would have been taken in the vicinity behind the old Sentinel Hotel, west of where the present Sentinel Bridge crosses the river. Notice that the water has risen almost to the top of the opening of the well.

Stereoview - **"Nature's Mirror, Yosemite Falls, California, U.S.A."**
Copyright 1902 by R. Y. Young American Stereoscopic Company
From author's collection.

In case you were wondering, there is a "Lake Yosemite". However, it is a reservoir near Merced, California, well outside Yosemite's boundaries.

"Mirror Lake, showing reflection of the Half Dome"

This photograph is from a 1919 booklet published by the United States Railroad Administration. The booklet was part of their National Park Series entitled *Yosemite National Park, California*.

While it is a very nice picture showing the reflective properties that Mirror Lake once had, the beautiful granite cliff seen in this picture is not Half Dome.

It is Mount Watkins. Viewed from this perspective, Half Dome would be to the right (out of the picture), across the canyon from where all the people are seen.

Postcard - **Mirror Lake and Mt. Wilson, Yosemite National Park**
From author's collection.

Whoops! Here's another misidentification of Mount Watkins. I don't know how someone thought this was Mount Wilson. There is no Mount Wilson in Yosemite National Park. Mount Wilson is one of the better known peaks in the San Gabriel Mountains, part of the Angeles National Forest in Los Angeles County, California. It is the location of the Mount Wilson Observatory.

Postcard – **Camp Curry - The Bathing Pool and Sentinel Dome, Yosemite Valley, California**
Detroit Publishing Company "PHOSTINT", #71354. Circa 1915 to 1930.
Courtesy of Dr. Paul P. Clark, *Adams Art* - researcher-collector-writer on Ansel Adams & Yo Semite.

Supposedly, the Sentinel Dome is shown in this postcard. The dome, however, that is pictured (top center) is actually the North Dome. The rock eddiface below and to the right of the North Dome is the Washington Column.

The Sentinel Dome can't be seen from Camp Curry, or Curry Village as it is now known. The view shown on the postcard would be towards the north-east, while the Sentinel Dome is to the south-west, about 3,500 feet above Yosemite Valley. And since Curry Village is located fairly close to the base of the cliff below Glacier Point, it's really hard to see much of anything except cliff if you look in any southerly direction.

Views of Yosemite by George Fiske, ca. 1880-1890, Identifier: 63
Title: [No Caption], Fiske identifier #484
Courtesy of The Bancroft Library. University of California, Berkeley.

Here is a beautiful landscape scene photographed by George Fiske showing a granite dome reflected in the placid water of a stream. The mirror image makes it so that it is difficult to distinguish which are the actual mountains and trees and which is the reflection.

And that is what is wrong with this picture.

This photograph was found on the California Digital Library, Online Archive of California (OAC), and a resource of the University of California Libraries. The photo is presented here, after some trimming of the borders, exactly as it appears online.

While it is definitely a beautiful scene somewhere in Yosemite, the problem is that online, the image is displayed upside-down. Here are detailed views of first the upper left-hand corner and then the upper right-hand corner –

This is an example of an easy mistake just waiting to happen.

On the next page is the photograph displayed properly with the signature "Fiske" in the lower right-hand corner and his identifying/stock number, #484, in the lower left.

Another clue as to which end is up (or down) is the gravel and sand seen where Fiske's signature appears, which is definitely not part of the reflective image.

Postcard – **View from Wawona Road – Yosemite**
From author's collection.

Let's say you're driving up Highway 41 from the Valley towards the Tunnel View. You're in a hurry to get to Wawona or Fresno and you don't have time to stop, but you would like to get one last look at the Valley. So you keep looking in the rear-view mirror. But you just can't get a nice, good, clear, memorable view before you get to the tunnel and the Valley is out of sight.

Has that ever happened to you? (Probably not, but for the sake of this postcard we'll say it has.)

Well, here's what it would look like if all that were possible – Yosemite Valley in your rear-view mirror - Bridal Veil Falls to the north, El Capitan on the south.

How did this one get past the editors?

Stereoview - **"Its Fleecy Whiteness Tinged with Emerald Green"**
Bridal Veil Falls, Yosemite Valley, Ca., U.S.A."
Keystone View Company.
Copyright 1897, by B. L. Singley
From author's collection.

There must have been some confusion created when the family and friends were gathered for the evening's entertainment of viewing the new set of stereoviews. While the caption on the front of this card identifies this as Bridal Veil Falls, the detailed description on the back states that this is a side view of Nevada Falls

> This picture shows a side view of Nevada Falls. As the traveler ascends the "Zigzags" leading to the top of Nevada Falls, he has every opportunity for seeing the magnificent effects in this falling water. The coruscations of light are resplendent as the sun's rays are reflected from this billowy mass of aerated water, and the rockets, the white ostrich plumes, and other forms, so often referred to, are seen in all their beautiful variety—surrounded by diamond spray and set in living green. The path is rocky and the climb is a steep one, but these effects, and the grandeur which awaits the traveler when the top of the Fall is reached, amply repay him for his perseverance.
> J. M. Hutchings, Author of "In the heart of the Sierras"

Which waterfall is it - Bridal Veil or Nevada?

Fortunately, there is additional evidence to help solve the mystery. A very similar photograph taken from the same perspective and about the same year helps identify the waterfall in question as Nevada Falls.

Just turn the page . . .

Nevada Fall
From an 8" x 10" glass transparency between 1890 and 1897, William Henry Jackson, photographer.
Part of Detroit Publishing Company Photograph Collection, Library of Congress Prints and Photographs Division
Call Number: LC-D4-6233, Reproduction Number: LC-USZ62-109709, Digital ID: det 4a28975

To help alleviate any further confusion in identifying which fall is which, I have provided the following photographs of Bridal Veil Falls taken from different perspectives.

What's Wrong With This Picture? - Yosemite National Park

All photographs of Bridal Veil Falls by author.
© 2012, Scott N. Tipton

I find it true myself, when seeing Yosemite Valley's more prominent waterfalls, especially in the spring, that the *"coruscations* of light are resplendent as the sun's rays are reflected from the billowy masses of aerated water"*. (In other words the falls are really beautiful, particularly when the blowing wind affects the movement of the cascades and creates a lot of mist.)

* There's a $3 word for you. It means flashes of light, like the sparkles and glitter of a cut diamond.

Stereoview - **"Mt. Lyell, Yosemite Valley"**
American Views
From author's collection.

Yosemite Valley, yes; Mt. Lyell, no.

Almost every other published photograph or picture of this scene correctly identifies the granite monolith rising in the background of this stereoview as Sentinel Rock. Sometimes this giant rock pillar was referred to as Loya (the name that some think the native people called it), Pyramid Rock or 'The Sentinel". By the time this photo was taken, circa 1866, Sentinel Rock was pretty much the name accepted by those who lived in Yosemite Valley.

While Sentinel Rock is an impressive and prominent feature of Yosemite Valley, Mount Lyell is an entire mountain, not a rocky crag. It would be difficult for an informed person to confuse the two.

The building in the foreground is the Hutchings' Hotel which was originally known as the Upper Hotel, and was built in 1857. There never was a hotel in the immediate vicinity of Mount Lyell, not closer than a day's mule ride, approximately.

I don't know how this image on a stereoview ended up with that caption, particularly since the same stereograph publisher, American Views, put out a very similar view card, which was a photograph taken from almost the exact same spot with the caption "Sentinel Rock, Yosemite". (see next page) The difference between the two photos is that the second stereoview shows the hotel at a slightly later date.

In a detail of the second stereoview, Sentinel Rock doesn't show up very clearly. By the time this photo was taken the hotel had a porch with an awning running over it and except for one small tree missing that appeared in the earlier photo, the basic scenery is the same.

At times there wasn't much research put into the production of stereoviews to sell to an unsuspecting public. It was sometimes more important to make sales and entertain than to educate.

Stereoview - **"Sentinel Rock – Yosemite"**
Zelda Mackay Collection of Stereographic Views
The Bancroft Library, University of California, Berkeley.

This is how the real Mt. Lyell looked before its glaciers began to melt and recede in the last few decades.

Postcard – **Mt. Lyell – Yosemite Nat'l. Park**
From author's collection.

Mt. Lyell is the highest peak in Yosemite National Park at an elevation of 13,114 feet (3,997 meters) and is located near the southeast boundary of the park.

Sentinel Rock has an elevation of 7,038 feet (a 6,076 foot difference) and is on Yosemite Valley's South side and is just west of the Sentinel Bridge.

Stereoview - **"First Hotel in Yosemite Valley, Cal."**
Popular Series stereoview.
From author's collection.

The building shown in the picture above was not the first hotel in Yosemite valley. It was not in the Park. It wasn't even a hotel!

This is just another example of someone having a picture that they wanted to sell in a set of stereoviews without caring to have all the facts. The photo *was* taken in California, the building *might* be a hotel, there are trees in the photo, and there are hotels and lots of trees in Yosemite, so, it just might as well be a hotel in Yosemite as anywhere else.

This very plain looking structure, however, was the first hotel built in Yosemite Valley –

The "Lower Hotel" circa 1860.
Courtesy Yosemite Research Library

In May of 1856, four gentlemen "took up a claim in Yosemite Valley and began living there." The men were John C. Anderson, of Illinois; A. Epperson, of Indiana; W. C. Walling, of Pennsylvania; and Judge Ben S. Walworth, of New York. They set up their camp on the south side of the Merced River, east of Sentinel Creek and below Sentinel Rock providing an excellent view of Yosemite Falls across the valley.

By July of that year the four men had "partially completed a frame house, which is to be enlarged and opened for the accommodation of visitors early next season." But the building was not finished that year. As a visitor in August reported he "found four men engaged in sawing lumber with a whip-saw for a house they intended erecting next spring for the accommodation of visitors . . . " *

By the spring/summer of 1857 this rough, 18 by 20 foot wooden building was finished enough to open for business. It wasn't much of a hotel however, as Galen Clark, an important individual In Yosemite's history, described it as "a saloon for the entertainment of that class of visitors who loved whisky and gambling."

Also in 1857, the construction of another structure was begun a little over half a mile eastward (upstream) on the south side of the Merced River. This hotel began as a blue canvas-covered building but in a few years was improved into a two story wooden structure.

Because of their proximity to each other, the first building, being downriver from the second, became commonly called the Lower Hotel. The second, somewhat newer building, being upstream, became known as the Upper Hotel.

During the winter of 1857/58 the original Lower Hotel was crushed by snow. It was rebuilt in 1858 by new owner/partners and over the next few years it functioned as a respectable inn, even though it looked like a barn and had its faults in regards to comfort and conveniences. Historian Shirley Sargent described the Lower Hotel this way –

* see Johnston, Hank 2006 'Yosemite's Pioneer Lower Hotel', *Yosemite* - A Journal for Members of the Yosemite Association, Winter 2006, Volume 68, Number 1, pp 3 - 6.

It looked like a barn, and its "rooms" resembled stalls. Windows were glassless, floors of dirt or pine boughs, and beds spring-less. Mattresses were ticking stuffed with hay, bracken, or some other soft material, and sanitary facilities consisted of a wash pan and a path. Chickens and cows outnumbered wild animals, and meadows had been planted to hay and grain. Comforts were at a minimum, but surrounding beauty so great that few lodgers complained. *

Improvements and additions were made to the hotel and there were changes in ownership and management as well. In 1869 the last lessees/managers, George and Isabella Leidig, opened their own two-story hotel, also on the south bank of the Merced River about one quarter mile west. The last owners of the Lower Hotel, Mr. and Mrs. Alex G. Black, then removed the old buildings and built 'Black's Hotel' in the original location. †

So, just what was that almost circular building with the domed roof mislabeled as being the first hotel in Yosemite Valley?

The building in question is actually a structure that was built on the stump of a giant sequoia tree in the Calaveras Big Tree Grove north of what became Yosemite National Park. It was a not a hotel but was used more as a dance hall and entertainment center.

The giant sequoia trees (*Sequoiadendron giganteum*) were first "discovered" in Calaveras County, California. When the existence of these giant trees became general knowledge beginning in June of 1852, a few greedy men thought of a way to exploit them for profit.

* YOSEMITE AND ITS INNKEEPERS - the story of a great park and its chief concessionaires, Copyright © 1975 by Shirley Sargent.

†The historical information pertaining to all the different individuals involved in owning, building, and managing the hotel(s) varies from account to account. The dates mentioned within these accounts for when these things occurred also are not always in agreement within a year or two. Therefore, this is a very short history of the hotel drawn from what I consider the most reliable sources.

In 1853, the first giant sequoia "discovered" the previous year, one of the largest of the trees in the Calaveras grove and called "The Discovery Tree" or "The Original 'Big Tree'", was cut down.

Some of its bark was stripped off in such a way that it could be reassembled to show how large the tree was. A cross-section was sawed off as well for the same purpose. These and other tree artifacts were shipped to New York and put on display to be viewed for the price of admission.

In New York the people that paid to see the "Original Big Tree" were generally of two opinions -

1. Most people did not think a tree of this size really existed. They suspected fakery and a hoax; that the displays were manufactured.

2. Or they were upset and angered that someone had cut down the "largest tree in the world", as it was advertised, to exploit it for profit.

The artifacts were accidently destroyed in a fire while they were in storage awaiting shipment to Paris.

It is extremely doubtful that the next photograph from a stereoview "Section of the Mammoth Tree, Cal." is the bark from "The Original Big Tree". The photographer, J. J. (John James) Reilly did not come to America from Scotland until 1856, almost three years after that tree was cut down. This photo is most likely the bark taken from another tree cut down around 1870 or later. But this photograph certainly gives an excellent idea of the appearance of what people saw when that first giant sequoia was cut down and the bark was taken off to be reassembled and displayed as an oddity.

Stereoview - **Section of the Mammoth Tree, Cal.**, by J. J. Reilly, Number 463
Stereographs of the West from the Bancroft Library Pictorial Collection, Identifier: 19xx.130:463
The Bancroft Library. University of California, Berkeley.

The stump and the remaining log sections of that "Original Big Tree" became part of the tourist attractions in the Calaveras Grove. The surface of the stump was smoothed and evened off so as to have a utilitarian purpose for visitors. James M. Hutchings, in his 1888 book In the Heart of the Sierras, describes that portion of the poor tree's remains as it appeared the year after it was felled -

BIG TREE STUMP.

This is the stump of the original Big Tree discovered by Mr. Dowd. We can see that it is perfectly smooth, sound, and level. Its diameter across the solid wood, after the bark was removed (and which was from fifteen to eighteen inches in thickness), is twenty-five feet; although the tree was cut off six feet above the ground. However incredible it may appear, on July 4, 1854, the writer formed one of a cotillion party of thirty-two persons, dancing upon this stump; in addition to which the musicians and onlookers numbered seventeen, making a total of forty-nine occupants of its surface at one time! The accompanying sketch was made at that time . . .

"A COTILLION PARTY OF THIRTY-TWO PERSONS DANCING ON THE STUMP OF THE MAMMOTH TREE."

Soon afterward, a pavilion was built over the stump. *That* is the building seen in the first photograph (page 183). Mr. Hutchings tells us that it was used "on Sundays in public worship; and on weekday evenings for dancing . . . Theatrical performances and concerts have taken place upon it; and, in 1858, the Big Tree Bulletin was printed and published here."

The original big tree, showing dancing hall on the Stump.
Calaveras big trees grove - 12 miles from Sheep Ranch.
Views of Calaveras and Mariposa Counties, No. 28, Identifier: 26
The Bancroft Library. University of California, Berkeley.

Stereoview – "**Sawing section of the Original. 98 ft. at base. [Yosemite Valley, California.]**"
Eadweard J. Muybridge, #119, 1868
Zelda Mackay Collection of Stereographic Views, Identifier: 16057
The Bancroft Library. University of California, Berkeley.

Stereoview – "**Interior of the house built on the Original Big Tree Stump, Calaveras County**"
Lawrence & Houseworth, Gems of California scenery, no. 909. Published 1866.
Library of Congress Prints and Photographs Division Washington, D.C. 20540 USA
LOT 3544-1, no. 909, LC-USZ62-27171, Control #: 2002722031

The destruction and exploitation of giant sequoia trees disturbed a great many people. What was done to "The Original Big Tree" as well as another giant sequoia in the Calaveras Grove a year later, "The Mother of the Forest", were contributing factors that lead to the passage of the Yosemite Land Grant of 1864. This effectively created the first National Park in the United States as a natural reserve.

Stereoview - **Mother of the Forest, 63 feet in circumference. Yosemite Valley, Cal.**
Copyright 1905, Kawin and Co.
"Reproduced from original stereoscopic photograph."
From author's collection.

This picture is one half of a lithographed stereoview of a giant sequoia tree that was dubbed the "Mother of the Forest". Actually, it is the trunk of what was once a huge living tree, one of the largest in the world.

The tree is not in Yosemite Valley. It is not in any of three groves of giant sequoia in Yosemite National Park. It is, however, in California and the "Mother of the Forest" has historical significance in relation to Yosemite.

Referring back to the information about the "First Hotel in Yosemite Valley", giant sequoia trees were "discovered" in Calaveras County, California in 1852.

As mentioned, what was considered the first tree discovered in the grove, variously called "The Discovery Tree" or "The Original Big Tree" was cut down in 1853 so that artifacts could be shipped around the country and displayed, the exhibitors making money on admission fees to see reassembled bark of the "world's largest tree." After the artifacts were displayed for awhile in New York City, they were put in storage to await shipment to Paris. The artifacts were destroyed by a fire before they could be shipped.

During the next year, 1854, someone else decided that they too could make money in a similar exploitation of another of the largest trees in the grove of giant sequoias. But instead of cutting down the chosen tree (it took over three weeks to fell the first tree with the tools available at the time) it was decided to just strip the bark off to put on display. This tree was known as the "Mother of the Forest".

Using scaffolding, the bark was removed in sections to the height of 116 feet, leaving the poor mammoth tree to slowly die. The remains became a very tall snag of dead wood - a sad memorial to the magnificent tree and a reminder of the results of greed and exploitation of some of nature's greatest beauty.

James M. Hutchings writing in his book "In the Heart of the Sierras" (1888) described what was done to this tree and included an illustration -

> The accompanying engraving, representing this once symmetrical tree, is from a daguerreotype taken in 1854, immediately after the bark was removed, and correctly represents the foliage of this wonderful genus, ere the vandal's "Effacing fingers had swept the lines where beauty lingers."

"MOTHER OF THE FOREST"
(321 feet in height, 84 feet in circumference, without the bark.)
Lithograph of the "Mother of the Forest" by J. C. Scripture from *In the Heart of the Sierras* by James M. Hutchings (1888).
Published at the Old Cabin, Yo Semite Valley and at Pacific Press Publishing House, Oakland, Cal., 1888.

The following photographs from vintage stereoviews depict the "Mother of the Forest". Notice the scaffolding used to remove the bark from the tree.

"Mother of the Forest; 305 ft. high; 63 ft. circumference; bark off 121 ft."
Half stereograph, albumen, published 1866.
Lawrence & Houseworth "Gems of California scenery" no. 888.
Library of Congress Prints and Photographs Division

Stereoview - **The Mother of the Forest, 305 ft high giant tree; 63 ft circumference--near view - Calaveras County.**
Lawrence & Houseworth, Gems of California scenery, no. 904. Published 1866.
Library of Congress Prints and Photographs Division

Stereoview - **"Mother of the forest" (90 ft.)--sacrificed to curiosity--died when bark (now in London) was stripped for exhibition, Calaveras Grove, Cal.**
Underwood & Underwood, publishers, c1902.
Library of Congress Prints and Photographs Division

The reassembled bark was on display in New York City and then the artifacts of this tree eventually made it to the Crystal Palace in London where in 1866, it also was lost to a fire.

Caption: "**The interior of the Tropical Transept looking along the Avenue of the Sphinxes to the Mammoth Tree, a sequoia from California, the original of which was 363 feet high and 4,000 years old.**"
Photographer: Philip Henry Delamotte, circa 1859.
The interior of the tropical North Transept contained a truncated version of a great Californian sequoia tree, the bark of which was supported by interior scaffolding. This had previously been displayed at the version of the Crystal Palace in New York. The tree was destroyed in the fire of 1866.
Philip Delamotte photographs of the Crystal Palace, Sydenham.
Photo used by permission.
© English Heritage.NMR
Reference Number: DP004612

The remains of the dead tree still exist in Calaveras Big Tree State Park, California.

Ironically this negative exploitation eventually brought about a few good results. Fortunately, there were people who wanted to protect and preserve the giant trees. When the Federal Government set Yosemite Valley aside for California to administer as a state park in 1864, the giant sequoias of the Mariposa Big Tree Grove were protected under the same legislation.

PART 4

IMPROVEMENTS BY DESTRUCTION AND DISTRACTION

There are three groves of Giant sequoia trees in Yosemite National Park.

The largest is the Mariposa Big Tree Grove. It was part of the Yosemite Land Grant of 1864 and is located in the southern part of the park. The other two groves, the Merced and Tuolumne, are located in the west-central part of the park, north of Yosemite Valley.

In the Tuolomne and the Mariposa groves different individuals at different times -- the real reasons only known to them -- cut tunnels through three of these giant trees big enough to drive carts, cararaiges and stage coaches through them.

For whatever reasons, nature could not be left alone and the sublime had to give way to novelty.

The first sequoia tree to meet this fate is in the Tuolumne Grove. Officially "discovered" on May 10, 1858, this grove contains about twenty-five large trees. One of the trees, originally named "King Solomon's Temple" is really more of a huge stump of what remains of the burned-up trunk. It is approximatley 90 feet tall and 29½ feet in diameter at the base (that's without any bark) and was also hollowed out by fire. Later the tree became called what it is still known as: "The Dead Giant."

Since one of the earliest roads from the north to Yosemite Valley, the Big Oak Flat Road, passed through this grove, someone had the novel idea of tunneling through the base of one of the trees. Some people just can't leave things as they find them. This was in 1878. Ten years later, James Hutchings described "The Dead Giant" in his book ***In the Heart of the Sierras*** this way:

> One of the most striking examples of the extraordinary growth of this species is found in the immense stump called "The Dead Giant," for, although fire has entirely denuded it of its bark, and largely reduced its proportions, it is even now thirty-one feet in diameter. By the earthy ridges that form around almost every forest tree, it is plainly evident that this, at one time, must have

had a circumference of over a hundred and twenty feet. For the purpose of enabling visitors more easily to apprehend its enormous size, a "tunnel" has been cut through it which is ten feet in width by twelve in height, and through which the stage coach passes when either going or returning to Yo Semite. There is no more convincing evidence of size than this in either of the groves . . .

In a later book, **The Big Oak Flat Road** (1955) by Irene D. Paden and Margaret E. Schlichtmann, it is stated "In order to force visitors to realize its size and to provide an additional point of interest, it was decided to tunnel the base of the trunk."

The first coach-load of travelers to experience the size of this tree by this means passed through the tunnel on Tuesday, June 18, 1878.

I'm not sure that the people who passed through the tunnel had a better understanding of how large the tree was compared to what they would have experienced had they stood next to it or walked around the base. But it was different.

The remains of "The Dead Giant" still stand, but you have to hike to the grove to see it. The main road no longer passes through the Tuolumne Grove.

DEAD GIANT, TUOLUMNE GROVE
Photograph by Boysen.
From *The Big Trees of California* (1907), by Galen Clark

THE DEAD GIANT (31 feet in diameter).
Photo by Geo. Fiske. Engraved by Heliotype Co., Boston.
From *In the Heart of the Sierras* by James M. Hutchings (1888)

The Dead Giant, Tuolumne Grove, 1894.
Photograph by Celia Crocker Thompson
From *The Big Oak Flat Road* (1959) by Irene D. Paden and Margaret E. Schlichtmann

What's Wrong With This Picture? - Yosemite National Park

Scott N. Tipton

Photos on previous page:

Upper left - WAWONA TREE, MARIPOSA GROVE.
Diameter, 28 feet; height, 260 feet; measured by Hon. B. M. Leitch, Guardian of the Grove.
Photograph by Boysen.

Upper right -WAWAWONA TREE, MARIPOSA GROVE, YOSEMITE NATIONAL PARK.
Photograph by Pillsbury Picture Co. Photograph by Pillsbury Picture Co.
From *The Secret of the Big Trees*
National Park Service

Lower left - National Park Service Photo.

Lower right - President Taft's Party at Wawona Tree, Mariposa Grove, 1900.
National Park Service Photo.

The second giant sequoia to have a tunnel cut through it was the Wawona Tree in the Mariposa Grove in 1881.

The Washburn Brothers, who owned the Wawona Hotel and the Yosemite Stage and Turnpike Company, as well as many other financial interests in the Yosemite area, had built a stage road to the Mariposa Grove. To advertise the road as well as "to give tourists the thrill of knowing the bigness of these trees", two brothers whose last name was Scribner were paid $75 to cut a tunnel big enough for the stage company's vehicles to take tourists through.

The tree chosen already had an old, large burn scar on it, which shortened the time needed to complete the job. The Wawona Tree was 234 feet tall. The tunnel itself was eight feet wide, twenty-six feet long and ten feet high.

It was such a strange way to get travelers to go look at these huge trees. One would think that people, as they do today, go to look at the trees just for the sake of seeing these wonders of nature; some of the largest living things on earth.

Cutting a tunnel through one of these giants of nature to help demonstrate how large they really are is like taking a one hundred dollar bill, using a big black pen to circle one spot where it says "One Hundred Dollars" and then "high-lighting" it as well for more emphasis. It's not necessary.

Poignant visual example:

Giant sequoia tree without tunnel.

Giant sequoia tree with tunnel.
Is the second bill more impressive?

Does spectacular nature such as this really need that something extra added to make it better? It may have made things a little more interesting, but certainly not any better.

Surprisingly, one of the 'discoverers' of the Mariposa Grove, Galen Clark, thought that the tunnel added something to the experience of seeing these massive trees. In his book *The Big Trees of California* (1907), he wrote that the Wawona Tree:

> . . . had been burned to such an extent that widening out the passage for stages did not injure the roots or vitality, and cannot properly be termed an act of spoliation or vandalism. A ride through these trees in a six-horse stage, or any conveyance, is a great novelty and should not be missed.

This statement was from the man whose job for many years was to protect and preserve the natural wonders as Guardian of the Yosemite Grant.

Cutting the tunnel through the Wawona Tree did create one of the biggest man-made tourist attractions of all time however. Not only did people want to ride a horse, carriage or coach through the tunnel, many wanted their photograph taken when they did so, which is easily seen from the illustrations. There have to be literally hundreds of thousands of photos like the ones seen on these pages. If nothing else, it was a boon to the professional photographers of the Yosemite area. In the book *Yosemite Indians and Other Sketches* (1936), Mrs. H. J. Taylor wrote:

> The advertisement brought returns and the route through the Mariposa Grove became popular. Driving through a tree with the stage was an interesting and thrilling experience. The photographer saw his opportunity; when the stage was almost through the tree it stopped; the camera man took the picture; the tourist gave orders for copies; and the stage drove on, and he awaited the next stage. Above the fireplace in the Yosemite Museum hangs a picture of one of the early stages driving through the Wawona Tree.

In this picture Galen Clark sits with the driver. Tourists in no small numbers drive through this tree each season.

In his 1949 book *A Guide to the Giant Sequoias of Yosemite National Park,* James W. McFarland wrote:

> The Wawona Tree has enjoyed more publicity than any other tree in the world. Hundreds of thousands of people visit it each summer. The question asked most frequently of the ranger naturalist at the museum is, "Where is the tree you can drive through?" . . . A favorite subject of artists and photographers alike, its portrait has been published in geography texts for over 50 years.

When the automobile replaced the horse and buggy, the tradition continued.

Unfortunately the poor giant fell over during the heavy winter snows of 1968/69. A publication by the National Park Service, *The Giant Sequoia of the Sierra Nevada** points out:

> The tree probably collapsed between February and May 1969 when, very fortunately, park visitors were not lined up bumper to bumper awaiting their turn to park in the tunnel and take the traditional photograph to be found in almost all geography books for nearly a century. Because of the unusually heavy snow during that winter, the crown may well have borne 1-2 tons of additional weight which the wood could not support.
>
> The lean of the famous Tunnel Tree in Yosemite National Park was surely part of its undoing, to say nothing of the tunnel cut through it in 1881 which weakened the tree much as a fire scar would.

* By, R. Hartesveldt, H. T. Harvey, H. S. Shellhammer and R. E. Stecker
San José University, California
U.S. Department of the Interior, National Park Service, Washington, D. C., 1975

No evidence supports the idea that its collapse was due to excessive trampling by people, the possible effects of which had earlier caused considerable concern (Hartesveldt 1963). Of course today, the cutting of the tunnel is looked upon as a sort of vandalism, and the tree very likely would still be standing had the tunnel never been cut.

The Giant Sequoias of California, Anderson Photo.
By Lawrence F. Cook, Chief of Forestry, National Park Service, 1955
United States Government Printing Office

This is how the Wawona Tree in Yosemite appeared before it fell over in a storm.
National Park Service Photo.

The remains of the Wawona Tunnel Tree following its collapse in 1969. After surviving 88 years of traffic passing through its well-known tunnel, it was felled by the rigors of winter.
Photo by R. J. Hartesveldt from *The Giant Sequoia of the Sierra Nevada*.

Thus ended the great adventure and learning experience that could be enjoyed by driving through a tunnel cut into a giant sequoia; in Yosemite National Park anyway.

But, as stated at the beginning of this section, there were three such trees in Yosemite.

The third "tunnel tree" was also in the Mariposa Grove, about one hundred yards east of the famous "Grizzly Giant." This tree was named the "California Tree." In 1895 a tunnel was cut through this 232 foot tall giant.

Why was there a need for two "Tunnel Trees" in the Mariposa Grove? I could not find a concrete reason for the California tree originally being cut through, but it worked out well in assuring there was a tunnel tree available to "experience" all the year round, which may have been the real reason.

Apparently, the Wawona Tree was not accessible all year round because in the winter snow and mud made the road to that tree inaccessible, so the California Tree became a back-up for those times. The *Yosemite Nature Notes* of April 1929 (Volume VIII, Number 4) explains:

> In that section of the Mariposa grove located about one hundred [yards] east of the ancient Grizzly Giant is to be found the California Tree. A tunnel was cut through the heart of this tree about 1895. A roadway was built so that passengers of the horse stages might be carried through a big tree in the Mariposa grove during that part of the season when snow and mud kept the road in a condition preventing travel into the upper grove and through the famous Wawona tree.

A Guide to the Giant Sequoias of Yosemite National Park (1949) by James W. McFarland tells us basically the same thing:

The old stagecoach road from the Grizzly Giant may be followed northeastward for about a hundred yards to the California Tree. It is one of the two living giant sequoias in the Mariposa Grove which has been tunneled. The cut was made in 1895. For many years it served as a substitute for the larger Wawona ("tunnel") Tree which became inaccessible when the winter snows blocked the road through the upper part of the grove.

It appears that going through a tunnel tree had become such an important part of one's visit to the Mariposa Grove that a back-up or substitute was needed in case the more famous one got snow bound.

The Wawona Tree was so famous that when coach drivers could not drive their passengers through it, they took them through the California Tree instead, and did not tell them it was a different tree. Sometimes ignorance is bliss.

There could be no more substitution or deception about the two trees after 1932 since the California Tree became inaccessible itself when the National Park Service realigned the roads in the grove. After the Wawona Tree fell in 1969 there was no more driving through any of the three tunnel trees in Yosemite.

Another strange chapter on man's trying to improve upon nature was brought to an end.

The California Tree.
A Guide to the Giant Sequoias of Yosemite National Park (1949) by James W. McFarland

Here are two examples of the California Tree being identified as the Wawona Tree.

Stereoviews from author's collection.

The "Firefall" or "Fire Fall"
Photograph public domain, owned by "Scfry".

Once upon a time, one of the nightly summer rituals in Yosemite was the man-made spectacle known as the Firefall. It was created by building a large fire up on the ledge of Glacier Point and then at a specified time the embers would be slowly pushed off the ledge producing what appeared as a waterfall of fire.

It is generally accepted that the Firefall began one night in 1872 when a local resident, James McCauley, pushed the remains of his campfire over the edge of Glacier Point. Visitors in the valley that saw it requested that it he do it again. The requests became so numerous that McCauley decided to charge $1.50 to produce each Firefall. This practice continued irregularly for a number of years.

McCauley built a hotel called the Mountain House on Glacier Point in 1878 which he and his wife operated each summer. On many nights McCauley would build a large campfire for his guests near the point of the granite cliff that jutted out over the Valley. They would sit around the fire and talk and sing. When everyone was ready to go back to the hotel, he would kick the coals off the edge of the cliff, thus producing the Firefall.

Later when his twin sons, John and Fred, attended school in Yosemite Valley, they would ride donkeys from the Mountain House down the Four Mile Trail. Before the return trip to Glacier Point the boys would request money from tourists to pay for the production of the Firefall and then gather firewood, load their donkeys with it, and make the return trip home to the hotel.

In 1898, the state commissioners who managed the Yosemite Grant evicted McCauley from the Mountain House when his lease expired thus ending the Firefall for a few years. McCauley's eviction was in favor of John F. Stevens who was in charge of transportation for the rich and influential Washburn brothers of Wawona.

In 1899, David and Jennie Curry established Camp Curry in Yosemite Valley at the foot of the cliff below Glacier Point. David Curry learned of the Firefall custom from visitors to his camp and decided to revive it on special occasions and for honored guests. He would occasionally send one of his employees up the treacherous Ledge Trail to build a large fire and push the embers off the cliff. Due to its popularity this was done more and more frequently until it became a nightly occurrence during Camp Curry's summer seasons.

Postcard – **"Camp Curry and Glacier Point, Yosemite, Cal."**
From author's collection.

Postcard from author's collection.

1944 Postcard – **The Fire Fall, Glacier Point, Yosemite National Park, California.**
Scenic View Card Co., # Y7
From author's collection.

An example of the pile of bark that would be ignited, allowed to burn down to embers and then pushed over the ledge. Photo from author's collection.

It also became ritualized during those summer months. There was nightly entertainment at Camp Curry and after the show, David Curry, who was proud of his loud, booming voice, would yell up the cliff "Hello, Glacier Point." The reply from above would be "Hello" or "Hello, Camp Curry" to which David Curry would yell "Let 'er go, Gallagher" and the Firefall would begin.

In 1913 the Firefall was discontinued by Adolph Miller, Assistant Secretary of the Interior, when David Curry tried to bully his way through lease and concessioner negotiations in Washington, D.C. Curry demanded a long-term lease, new privileges within the park and permission to expand his camp. Mr. Miller responded:

> "We are not going to do anything for you. I'm not going to give you anything you ask for. Furthermore, I'm going to take something away from you. I hope you will learn from what we are going to do here, because you just can't go along the way you are now and expect to be a concessionaire. . . . I'm going to take the Firefall away. There will be no Firefall."

After that incident, David Curry would begin the nightly entertainment program at Camp Curry by saying "Welcome to Camp Curry, where the Stentor [Curry] calls and fire *used* to fall."

In 1917, Secretary of the Interior Franklin K. Lane granted the Curry Camping Company a five-year lease and said that the Firefall could be reinstated as a nightly summertime event. And so the man-made attraction continued for many years after that.

Postcard – **"Campfire Entertainment, Camp Curry, in the Yosemite National Park."**
From author's collection.

The ritual of the Firefall had some changes made over the years. At Camp Curry, the nightly entertainment would end at 9:00PM and the rite would begin. There would be signals by flashlights between Camp Curry and the top of Glacier Point. Then an employee with a loud voice would yell:

"Hello, Glacier Point."

From Glacier Point: "Hello, Camp Curry."

From Camp Curry: "Is the fire ready?"

Reply from Glacier Point: "The fire is ready."

From Camp Curry: "Let the fire fall."

Reply from Glacier Point: "The fire falls."

Next the embers from the large fire started a few hours earlier would be slowly pushed over the ledge with a special rake to create the desired waterfall effect that would last for some minutes. At Camp Curry while the glowing embers fell the "Indian Love Call" (from the Broadway musical and movie "Rose Marie") was sung as the visitors enjoyed the sight of what seemed to be a waterfall of fire. Many would be moved to tears. Afterwards the tourists could enjoy dancing at the Pavilion or go to a movie.

Postcard – **"Yosemite National Park, California – The Fire on Glacier Point"**
From author's collection.

At the campgrounds where Ranger-Naturalists would be giving nightly lectures, the Rangers had to be sure to be finished by 9:00 so the audience could watch the Firefall. "America the Beautiful" was played, and the audience sang along.

Postcard – **"Yosemite National Park, California – The Fire Fall, Glacier Point"**
From author's collection.

The Firefall was also done in the winter months when the Yosemite Park and Curry Company, Yosemite's main concessioner at the time, was trying to promote and attract visitors to new winter activities such as ice skating, tobogganing and skiing at Badger Pass.

But there are enough natural attractions and wonders in Yosemite that man-made attractions such as the Firefall are not necessary. It was not educational, but merely a nightly entertainment event that was finally ended after many decades.

In January of 1968, George Hertzog, Director of the National Park Service, ordered that the Firefall be discontinued. There were two main reasons. The first was that the Firefall was a man-made event, which detracted from National Park Service policy to encourage appreciation of natural wonders. It was just out of place.

The second was that over the years as Yosemite attracted more and more visitors, excessive environmental damage, especially to the meadows in eastern Yosemite Valley, was occurring due to the large crowds that gathered in the meadows to watch the Firefall. There had been 2.8 million visitors to the park in 1967 alone. People were not just trampling the meadows to get a view of the Firefall; they were parking their cars in them as well. In addition, major traffic jams occurred while everyone stopped to watch. As Alfred Runte put it in his book *YOSEMITE – THE EMBATTLED WILDERNESS*: the Firefall simply attracted too many spectators who brought too many cars and left behind too much litter, automobile exhaust, and trampled vegetation.

There are many instances written where Mr. Hertzog is said to have made a statement like the following: "if people want to see something like that, they could go to Disneyland." I could not substantiate that remark.

However, the Assistant Park Superintendent at the time did state that:

> It is a kind of travesty on nature to push glowing embers over the cliff when Yosemite provides such great natural spectacles. It is an artificial spectacle which could better be held at the county fairgrounds.

The last Firefall was on Thursday, January 25, 1968, when, because it was Winter, there was no crowd.

I saw the Firefall many times; it was pretty, absolutely spectacular. But I agree with the National Park Service's decision to end the show. I know that many people do not.

To this day when my wife and I visit Yosemite, I still hear other visitors ask "What happened to the Firefall?" On nature walks, at the Visitors' Center and at evening interpretation programs they say "What happened to the Firefall? I wish they never stopped it."

It's time to let it go and just accept that it's gone.

PART 5

THE ODD, STRANGE AND SILLY

"In the Heart of the Sierras"
From a painting by Charles Dormon Robinson.

This picture (see previous page) appeared opposite the title page of the 1888 book *In the Heart of the Sierras** by James Hutchings.

James Mason Hutchings was very familiar with Yosemite and its environs. He was with one of the first parties to visit Yosemite Valley purely as tourists in 1855, was a long time hotel keeper there, wrote extensively about Yosemite and was the Guardian of the Yosemite Grant for the State of California from 1880 until 1884.

The picture's artist, Charles Robinson (1847 – 1933), first visited Yosemite in 1880 and spent his summers there for the next twenty-four years. So, he also was very familiar with the scenery there.

If someone wanted to cram most of what makes Yosemite famous into one picture, this is a good effort. Here is a grizzly bear on an overhanging rocky projection, a giant waterfall, enormous cliffs, El Capitan, Half Dome and the High Sierras in the distance all rolled into one, and all pretty much out of proportion.

Just where in Yosemite do you go to see this? One of the only things missing from this picture is a Giant Sequoia tree.

The beauty of Yosemite is incredible and fantastic just as it appears. Why would someone painting or writing about the beautiful things to be seen and experienced in Yosemite need to depict such a fictitious scene? Wouldn't the view from Inspiration Point in and of itself be spectacular enough?

It seems that for some people nature as it appears is not quite enough but needs to be more impressive; as if it should be exaggerated and improved. This is a good example. I just might steal it for my company logo.

---

*In the Heart of the Sierras; the Yo Semite Valley, both historical and descriptive: and Scenes by the Way. Big Tree Groves. The High Sierra, with its Magnificent Scenery (etc.) By J. M. Hutchings, of Yo Semite. Published at the Old Cabin, Yo Semite Valley, and at Pacific Press Publishing House, Oakland, Cal. 1888

What's Wrong With This Picture? - Yosemite National Park

Yosemite Nature Notes, Volume XXXVII (37), Number 1, January 1958, page 14.

The caption on this photo is –

OUT OF YOSEMITE'S PAST
A One Picture Story

At the turn of the century pagents [*sic*] were popular in Yosemite. Just what was being portrayed here at Mirror Lake is lost to time unless some reader may have the answer.

Just what is being portrayed is still a mystery. But thanks to Linda Eade, Librarian of the Yosemite Research Library, the mystery of who is posing so artfully is now solved.

The woman so creatively poised is Ruth St. Denis, a famous dancer of the early 1900's and a contemporary of Isadora Duncan. She was known for her modern, dramatic style which she based on her interpretations of the Eastern history, culture, religion and mythology of Japan, India and Egypt. Her modern choreography with exotic costumes were known as "dance translations" and "music visualization".

Around 1921 Miss St. Denis and her husband and dancing partner Ted Shawn were in Yosemite Valley to perform a dance recital titled "Valse Directoire" (later known as "Josephine and Hippolyte"). It was apparently at this time that Ruth St. Denis had this and other photographs taken of herself in costumes at various locales in Yosemite Valley. Ted Shawn also had several photographs taken of himself in costume as an American Indian performing something called "Invocation to the Thunderbird".

(Rather strange stuff indeed. If you ever get a chance, check out the New York Public Library's on-line photography collection of Ms. Denis and Mr. Shawn. Remember that art is in the eye of the beholder; or in the mind of the performer.)

Yosemite Nature Notes, Volume XXXVI (36), Number 9, September 1957, page 97.

The caption on this photo is -

    OUT OF YOSEMITE'S PAST - A One Picture Story
    Part of the Cast of "Ersa". 1925. Who remembers?

Thanks once again to Linda Eade, librarian of the Yosemite Research Library, for shedding light on the scene depicted above.

Back in the 1920's the National Park service included as part of its educational work "the staging of historical and allegorical pageants." Beginning in about 1920 in the Giant Forest of Sequoia National Park, there was the staging of an annual play entitled "Ersa of the Red Trees." The play was to inspire in its viewers an appreciation for the preservation of the Giant Sequoias.

Plays and pageants were felt to be such an important educational tool that in 1925 the National Park Service appointed Garnet Holme, an English actor/director/writer who had immigrated to California, as official "Pageant Master."

More about what the preceding photo is about is explained in the *ANNUAL REPORT OF THE DIRECTOR OF THE NATIONAL PARK SERVICE* - Department of The Interior, National Park Service, Washington, D. C., October 4, 1926. Under the heading "NATIONAL PARK PAGEANTS" is the following information -

> Another interesting phase of educational work in the national parks and monuments is the staging of historical and allegorical pageants. The first of these to be presented this year [1925] was "Ersa of the Red Trees," presented in the Mariposa Grove of Yosemite National Park. This play is an appeal for the preservation of the noble Sequoia trees, and has been given previously in the Giant Forest of Sequoia National Park. Another great open-air pageant was presented in the Yosemite in connection with the diamond jubilee anniversary of the park's discovery and depicted the history of the valley during the past 75 years.
> (See "Tenaya" in next reference)

More information is found in the book *"Oh, Ranger!" A Book about the National Parks* (Copyright 1928 by Horace M. Albright and Frank J. Taylor 1928, 1929, Stanford University Press)

> The national park pageants, most of which were developed by the late Garnet Holme, former pageant master of the National Park Service, preserve much of our Indian lore. Tenaya, a pageant of Yosemite named after he Indian chief who ruled Yosemite Valley when the white men came, pictures the wresting of the famous valley from the Indians. Ursa of the Redwoods [sic] enacts the legends of the giant redwoods in Sequoia National Park. Casa Grande pictures the ceremonies by which the desert Indians of Arizona and New Mexico sent their prayers to the rain gods. In all of these out-of-door dramas, Mr. Holme has delved into history and attempted to preserve the

legends and the true stories of the Indians as nearly as can be done. Another fine pageant is The Masque of the Absaroka, presented by the people of Bozeman, Montana, preserving legends of the Crows. The National Park Service has encouraged these pageants as a means of reviving the picturesque and interesting Indian ceremonies, one of the first features of Indian life to disappear when the native adopts the white man's mode of living.

While I could find very little information about "Ersa of the Big Trees" or how the production enacted "the legends of the giant redwoods," I did find more about the pageant "Casa Grande", which was held in Casa Grande National Monument. Here is an example of what one of Garnet Holme's pageants was like –

> The subject of a pageant first surfaced in May 1922 when the Women's Clubs of the towns of Florence and Casa Grande met at the monument to discuss ways to give the ruins more publicity. They decided that one means to get people to come to the monument from long distances would be to hold a pageant.
>
> Garnet Holme, the National Park Service pageant director, was chosen to supervise the play. He came to the monument in November 1925 to "gather impressions" for the pageant which was scheduled to be held in November 1926.
>
> A cast of 300 persons was selected and a three-day production was chosen for November 5-7, 1926. The pageant consisted of four dramas which had little connection to either the prehistory or history of the monument . . . The first episode told the "tragic" story of prehistoric Pueblo Indians who had been driven from their homes. This was followed by a Pima production of songs, dances, and rituals that ended when Coronado arrived. Angered at not finding gold, Coronado destroyed the Pima village. In the third part Padre Kino appeared on stage as the first European visitor to the abandoned ruins. He came to bring God and learning to the "superstitious" and

"illiterate" savages. Finally, the actors performed "beautiful Spanish love songs and fandangos" to show the "gaiety and revelry" of Spanish life in the Tucson of old.*

Just a reminder, this pageant supposedly depicted "the ceremonies by which the desert Indians of Arizona and New Mexico sent their prayers to the rain gods."

I can only imagine that "Ersa of the Red Trees" was similar in nature when it came to production value, even if it was a popular and successful pageant in Sequoia National Park and was well accepted in Yosemite.

In Greek mythology, Ersa (or Hersa) was the Greek goddess of the dew. She was the daughter of Zeus and Selene, the goddess of the moon. That's not a Native American tale or legend, and I don't know how Greek mythology ties into the story of the giant sequoias. But, just like "Casa Grande", "Ersa of the Red Trees" probably "had little connection to either the prehistory or history" of the giant sequoias.

Garnet Holme's pageantry lives on in Yosemite even today. In 1927 when the Ahwahnee Hotel was completed, Holme was hired to create a grand Christmas celebration for the hotel - The Bracebridge Dinner. Although altered over the years, it is still a popular annual event.

---

* Casa Grande Ruins
National Monument, Arizona: A Centennial History of the First Prehistoric Reserve 1892 – 1992
By A. Berle Clemensen, March 1992
An Administrative History
United States Department of the Interior/National Park Service

Stereoview - **A majestic triumphal arch – cavalry passing through the great tree "California" – Cal.**
© Underwood & Underwood, (15) -5976
No copyright year.
From author's collection.

Yosemite became an official National Park under the "California Forest Reservation Act of 1890" on October 1 of that year. This created a national park with unique situations.

The first was that the Yosemite Land Grant of 1864 had already set aside Yosemite Valley and the Mariposa Grove of Big Trees as protected lands under the control of the State of California. They remained under the jurisdiction of the State until 1906, when those lands were ceded back to the control of the U.S. Government. During that time period Yosemite Valley, the state controlled park, was surrounded by the official U.S. National Park with the Mariposa Grove, also still under state control, just outside the boundaries to the south.

The second unique situation was that while the new National Park was under the jurisdiction of the Secretary of the Interior there was no provision made for how he was to carry out the enforcement of the provisions of Section 2 of that Act:

> . . . for the preservation from injury of all timber, mineral deposits, natural curiosities, or wonders within said reservation, and their retention in their natural condition . . . against the wanton destruction of the fish, and game found within said reservation, and against their capture or destruction, for the purposes of merchandise or profit. He shall also cause all persons trespassing upon the same after the passage of this act to be removed therefrom, and, generally, shall be authorized to take all such measures as shall be necessary or proper to fully carry out the objects and purposes of this act.

Following the example of what had been done in regards to Yellowstone National Park after its establishment in 1872, the U.S. Army was called upon to provide protection and enforce rules and regulations.

So beginning in 1891, usually from the months of May through September when the tourist visitation was the heaviest, troops from the Presidio of San Francisco served as the official administrators with the commanding officer of the troops presiding as Acting Superintendent of Yosemite and Sequoia National Parks until 1914 .

Like many tourists to the area they had their photo taken at one of the well known landmarks, this one being the "California Tree", one of the two "tunnel trees" in the Mariposa Grove. The best known of the two trees was the "Wawona Tree" which was probably the most photographed tree in the world.

There are two anomalies with this picture. The first is that the Mariposa Grove was not under the jurisdiction of the U.S. troops. The State of California Yosemite Commissioners had control of that area, so the cavalry was just there for the photo opportunity.

The second oddity is the trooper third from the left in the front row.

Either this was Trooper John "Baby Face" Smith, or one of the regular Army personnel's children. He appears to be between ten to twelve years old.

Stereoview - **Troop I, 15th Cavalry on the trunk of the "Fallen Monarch," Mariposa Grove, California.**
Copyright 1901 by Underwood & Underwood
From author's collection.

The preceding photos may help us at least to identify the Reginent of cavalry that appear in the first two pictures.

The 15th Cavalry was indeed assigned to duty in Yosemite under the command of Major Louis Aleck Craig from June 17 to September 10, 1901. However official records indicate that it was Troop "H", not "I", that patrolled the park that year.

On close examination Trooper John "Baby Face" Smith may be seen astride his horse, fourth from the left, on top of the dead trunk of the "Fallen Monarch."

At least this time he doesn't appear to be armed, unless he's carrying a pistol.

O.K., one last look at this kid in the cavalry -

Stereoview - **Grizzly Giant, the largest living Tree in the World, Mariposa Grove, California.**
Copyright 1901 by Underwood & Underwood
From author's collection.

The picture may be a bit fuzzy, but you can tell it's the same kid, with his arms crossed. His trademark look seemed to be his hat with the brim turned up in the front.

That must have been one great summer for that young man. Imagine getting to hang out with a troop of cavalry for three months in one of the most beautiful places on earth. Sometimes being an Army brat had its privileges.

Photo from author's collection.

This is a photograph of Troop "F" of the 6th Cavalry. They were in Yosemite from August 3 to October 18, 1899. Their commanding officer was Captain Elon Willcox which made him Acting Superintendent of the national park for that summer.

As with the previous photos of the cavalry in the Mariposa Grove, it was the thing to do to have your picture taken next to or on a well known landmark. Again, this troop chose the famous "Fallen Monarch." This was a very popular photo opportunity because on the other side of the fallen tree trunk there were steps built so you and your horse, or buggy, or automobile (with a ramp) could get up on the log for that souvenir picture.

Similarly, there is a person one would not usually associate with a group of soldiers out patrolling and doing law enforcement detail for a few months, particularly when "roughing it."

This time it is a woman. Maybe she just was just visiting her husband, father or brother. Maybe she had come out with the troops and stayed with her husband the entire tour of duty. It would be hard to know what the circumstances really were, but there she is, on the top of the roots, center stage.

Based on the next photograph, I have a feeling she was Mrs. Willcox, since the picture appears to have been taken the same time as the first. I am assuming that her position in the photo directly above the gentleman in the officer's uniform would mean she had some relation to him. And since the officer is at the head of the column I also make the assumption that he is the commander, Captain Willcox.

It's like something out of a John Ford movie with John Wayne and Maureen O'Hara like "Rio Grande": the lone woman struggling with the hardships she faces for the man she loves, while the man's first love is the U.S. Cavalry.

The Fallen Monarch with Troop F, Sixth Cavalry, U.S.A. Mariposa Big Tree Grove California.
Yosemite National Park, Photographer: H. C. Tibbitts. Copyright © 1899, Southern Pacific Company.
National Park Service Historic Photograph Collection. Catalog Number: HPC-000602.

I have seen a few other photographs of the cavalrymen in Yosemite accompanied by women, but I have only one other in my personal collection.

This one is from a stereoview of the 9th Cavalry. The 9th Cavalry was a "Colored" regiment made up of African-American enlisted men, often referred to as "Buffalo Soldiers."

Many of these men had served in the Southwest U.S. in the "Indian Wars" against the Cheyenne, Apache, Kiowa, Ute, Comanche, and Sioux. The long timers and "lifers", after that, fought in the Spanish-American War of 1898 in Cuba and then in 1899 and 1900 were sent to the Philippines to fight the "insurrectionists."

Stereoview - **Troop D, 9th Cav., on the trunk of the Fallen Monarch, Mariposa Grove, Cal. U.S.A.**
Copyright 1905 by H. C. White Co.
From author's collection.

In this photo two women can be seen, one at the end, far right; the other is third from the right.

The caption for the stereoview from which this picture is derived says that this is Troop "D" but official records indicate only Troops "K" and "L" of the 9th Cavalry served in Yosemite. Also, while the copyright for the stereoview is 1905, the 9th Regiment served in Yosemite in the summers of 1903 and 1904.

If the photograph was actually taken in 1904, the Commanding Officers would have been either Major John Bigelow, Jr. (May 23 to September 25, 1904) or Capt. Willard Herman McCornack (September 25 to December (?), 1904).

The women were most likely wives and/or daughters of officers.

Postcard - **A Yosemite Chief, in the Yosemite National Park.**
Copyright by and Published Exclusively for Camp Curry Studio in the Yosemite National Park, California, by E. C. Kropp Co., Milwaukee, Wis. From author's collection.

I'm trying to imagine what the reaction of any visitor in Yosemite would have been if a man dressed up like the one on the previous page suddenly came popping out of the bushes. Mom would faint and the kids would run away in all directions, screaming at the top of their lungs. If Dad didn't have a heart attack, he would start to beat the "Chief" with his hiking staff to defend his family and himself.

I'm not too sure that it would be very often that tourists would see some white guy dressed up in "Indian" garb come scrambling out of the shrubbery, even the "Chief." What would be the point?

Postcard folder from author's collection.

Here is an early example of a souvenir folder of postcard-type color tinted pictures. Usually the pictures that were contained in folders such as this were available as individual postcards. The publisher just put together a set of their postcards, usually in a strip that folded accordion style. Sometimes the sets were individual, single postcard-like pictures. These folder/mailers were very popular for many years and similar newer sets can still be purchased.

This one is fairly early and was mailed in 1914. There is nothing unusual about the front or address side of this folder. It has a nice depiction of a wagon-load of people passing through the Wawona Tree in the Mariposa Grove, probably one of the most popular Yosemite photographs of the time.

There is something quite unusual about the back of this particular folder. Instead of another popular view of what one could expect to see in Yosemite, like Half Dome, El Capitan or one of the famous waterfalls, there was this amazing drawing:

There is so much that is wrong with this picture I don't know where to start. And, couldn't the artist at least have drawn a *smiling* Indian?

Postcard - **"Beezle Bill"**

Postcard - **"Jimmy Seekoya"**

What's Wrong With This Picture? - Yosemite National Park

Postcard - **"Muletta"**

Postcard - **"Peach-A-Rilla"**

Postcard - **"Yosemite Zip"**
All postcards from author's collection.

Once upon a time, a thirty-five year-old man by the name of Herbert Sonn came to Yosemite. The year was 1914. Mr. Sonn wrote a letter to his family in Newark, New Jersey and in it made this statement: "Send my things. I'm going to stay."

Being creative and artistic, Herbert Sonn would take easily found natural items and make whimsical and fictitious forest creatures out of them. Known as "Wild Gazoobas", his creations as well as picture postcards of them were sold in Yosemite gift shops and were his main source of income.

His creativity can be seen in the materials used to make his little creatures - walnuts, almonds, filberts, acorns, peach pits, cones of firs and giant sequoias, pine cone scales, sticks, stems, gnarled roots, bits of bark, feathers and moss. Put together in the right way with his imagination and you've got a cute little "bird" or "animal."

He first lived in Yosemite Valley in an area known as Kenneyville where livery stables, tack shops and some housing were located until 1926 when the buildings were torn down to make way for the construction of the Ahwahnee Hotel.

After that he lived in an area of Camp Curry. He set up two tents, one for living quarters and the other for a business office. He also had a cleared out area in which he set up chairs where visitors could listen to his lectures and observe demonstrations concerning the birds and animals of Yosemite. He was so natural in his interaction with the birds, and they so at ease with him, that he became known as the Bird Man.

During the tourist season he would put on two "shows" every afternoon at his campsite. He was also an expert at birdcalls. The birds would gather round him, even land on him, and he would describe their traits and habits. After the shows he would sell his little Wild Gazooba caricatures and postcards. He was actually one of Yosemite's earliest naturalist/interpreters.

Mr. Sonn made and sold his little characters and gave his nature lectures until he retired and moved from Yosemite Valley in 1937.

Herbert Sonn at his lodging at Kenneyville.
Courtesy of the Yosemite Research Library.

The Bird Man's camp in Camp Curry.
From author's collection.

Herbert Sonn with two Steller's Jays and one Wild Gazooba.
Courtesy of the Yosemite Research Library.

AFTERTHOUGHTS

I hope you have enjoyed my collection of fictitious, erroneous, silly, dangerous and strange pictures. I also hope that you found it educational.

The National Parks have been a long term experiment in preservation and protection of America's natural wonders and environment for the enjoyment of the people of the world. Along the way many things have occurred and been allowed that today would not be. This has been due largely to ignorance and/or trying to provide the best experience for the visitor to the parks.

Administering the National Parks is not an easy task. One of my favorite quotes concerning the job is by Charles Goff Thomson who was Yosemite's superintendent from 1929 to 1937. He summarized very well what is involved in trying to manage the National Parks, Monuments and Wild Lands:

> Simplified to the ultimate terms, we face two rather conflicting necessities:
>
> First, the National Park Service is controlled by an earnest determination to preserve the parks for posterity; every responsible officer is determined to turn over to the next generation a finer Yosemite than we inherited - - a Yosemite not ruined by over-development, a Yosemite with all its natural features preserved, it's wonderful forests unravaged, its wildlife influenced as little as possible, its wilderness as untouched as possible. There is no false conception that we can or should fix the character of its use permanently, for succeeding generations will know better how to adapt these priceless areas to their needs; but we owe it to future generations not to over-develop the area; not to mar any essential beauties; not to permit exploitation in any form; to safeguard against destructive nibbling processes. National parks are not Coney Islands, but distinctive idealistic American institutions. They are not resorts - - not areas for promotion, but for conservation.

> Our second responsibility, fully as important and more immediate, is to make Yosemite as useful as possible to the people of this generation, to enrich the lives of its users to the greatest possible extent.
>
> Historic Resource Study - YOSEMITE: THE PARK AND ITS RESOURCES - A History of the Discovery, Management, and Physical Development of Yosemite National Park, California Volume 1 of 3 - Historical Narrative by Linda Wedel Greene, September 1987, U.S. Department of the Interior / National Park Service

It has not been, is not now, nor will it ever be an easy task to make Yosemite National Park what it was meant to be - a place "for public use, resort and recreation . . . inalienable forever."

All of us who love and enjoy Yosemite can do our part individually to ensure that it remains as we would like it to be.

I see it very simply: Be part of the solution, not part of the problem.

This way, hopefully, your next visit to Yosemite will be as enjoyable an experience as the last.

And the next generation can learn from our example and do the same.

What's Wrong With This Picture? - Yosemite National Park

ABOUT THE AUTHOR

Scott Tipton has been visiting Yosemite National Park since 1959. He has an absolute passion about the park. His wife and he try to visit Yosemite at least once a year. They enjoyed camping at the Lower River campground until the flood of 1987 destroyed both Upper and Lower River campgrounds. Since the National Park Service decided not to re-open those campgrounds, they now stay at Curry Village when they visit.

When in Yosemite, the author enjoys waking early, taking his camera and a cup of coffee and walking through the Curry Village parking lot looking to see if any cars had been broken into by bears. (Everybody needs a hobby.) He then walks around Stoneman Meadow to see what wildlife may be out and about. He spends as much time as possible hiking and taking unnecessary risks to take photos. A lot of time is also spent at the Research Library digging through the photograph files looking for pictures to use in his writing projects, hanging out at the Ahwahnee hotel reading and attending the interpretive programs every night.

He also has a compulsion about collecting memorabilia, books and ephemera relating to Yosemite. That compulsion led to the writing of this book. It was an endeavor to look at Yosemite National Park by means of a collection of antique and vintage lithographs, paintings, photographs, postcards and stereoviews that just aren't right. He has another more serious history book about Yosemite in the works, as well as plans to write a biography about James Hutchings, a pioneer settler and hotel owner in Yosemite Valley.

Any comments or questions about this book or Yosemite National Park can be sent to the author at sntipton@everythingyosemite.com.